Benefits of His Passion

Bill Spaid
May 1989

Benefits of His Passion

Reflections on the Gospel of John
(Chapters 10–19)

Desmond Hunt

for
weekly Bible study
or
daily Lenten devotion

Anglican Book Centre
Toronto, Canada

1986
Anglican Book Centre
600 Jarvis Street
Toronto, Ontario
Canada   M4Y 2J6

Typesetting by Jay Tee Graphics
Printed and bound in Canada by John Deyell Company

Canadian Cataloguing in Publication Data

Hunt, Desmond.
  Benefits of His Passion

ISBN 0-919891-32-2

1. Bible. N.T. John X-IXX - Meditations. 2. Jesus
Christ - Passion -Meditations. 3. Devotional
- literature. I. Title.

BS2615.4.H86 1986   226′.5   C86-093229-X

to my wife Naomi
who is a constant source of encouragement
and who gave this book its title

Contents

Preface

These brief studies in John's gospel were originally intended to encourage meditation during the Lenten season and have been arranged with the Lenten days in mind. But there is a growing demand for material for study groups where reflection, discussion, and sharing are valuable anytime. Some will find this set of studies useful for this purpose.

The sections are designated both by numbers (for consecutive weekly study during the year), and by days (for daily devotion during Lent). However they are used, it is my hope and prayer that they will encourage us to read carefully some of the old familiar passages and find new blessing and hope.

Desmond C. Hunt

1 Ash Wednesday

John 10:1–10

It seems to be the unanimous consent of shepherds and sheep farmers that sheep are extraordinarily self-willed and thick-headed. I visited a sheep farm about a year ago and was told by the shepherd that he never ceases to be amazed at how ill-equipped sheep are to take care of themselves. They can drown in an inch of water. They can stray irresponsibly and lose all touch with the flock. They are helpless without a shepherd.

When the prophet Isaiah said, "All we like sheep are gone astray; we have turned everyone to his own way," he must have had some experience with sheep. But he also showed some very real understanding of human nature. It is not easy for us to respond positively to his assessment. We have developed impressively in the area of technical knowledge. We can transplant parts of the body. We can put two men on the moon. And we can sit in our living room and watch it happen. The capacity of the human mind is wonderful.

And yet Jesus has no hesitation in comparing men and women to sheep needing a shepherd. We are marvellously skilful in building a house but woefully inadequate in building a home. We are well equipped to build a city, but we stumble and falter in building a community. We act as sheep without a shepherd.

Now, there are many would-be shepherds. These are people who offer leadership. But their motives are not always pure, and they cannot always be trusted. Sheep are not discerning and will follow almost any voice. One has only to read the history and follow the current upsurge of many cults to realize the strong following given to modern shepherds and would-be saviours. The true shepherd brings his sheep in and out by the door. We need to remember that in the East there is no door to a sheepfold. The shepherd herds his sheep into a pen and then lies across the doorway and becomes the door himself. "I am the door," says Jesus, and to enter one must come in by way of him.

Here then is the picture of the family of God. We are led in by way of Jesus Christ. We are baptized into his name and meet in fellowship with others who bear and trust his name. We go out into the market-place bearing his name and reflecting his life and his love. He calls us all by name. In this day of anonymity and impersonal identity, when we are asked to produce not our name but our social security number or our driver's license number, it is good to hear and be known in the family of God by our name. It is a sign of belonging and being loved by the good and true shepherd — even Jesus Christ.

For reflection

People generally look upon themselves with optimism. They like to think of themselves as self-assured and independent. Jesus looked upon people as sheep needing a shepherd. How do you respond to his assessment of us?

2   Thursday

John 10:11-18

What do you expect of life? The Americans talk about the pursuit of happiness but discover that happiness is a very illusive commodity indeed. The Third World would answer in terms of material subsistence or freedom of conscience. Some people who have all this are in confusion as to what to expect of life. They try the route of artificial pleasure with drugs or alcohol. And they experience only deeper disillusionment.

Jesus says, "I came that they may have life, and have it abundantly." He is speaking of a life that is full and fulfilling. It is a life where you find yourself becoming what you were intended to be. It is a life not determined by circumstances at all. You find people who are invalid as well as strong. You find people in prison as well as free. St Paul tells of his experience of this abundant life in 2 Corinthians 6:4-10. Actually, abundant living is finding out who you are and where you came from, and why you are here and where you are going. It is life which men and women long for. For when Jesus said, "I have come to give you abundant life," he must have struck a responding chord.

Life with a good shepherd is depicted for us in Psalm 23. It is the best possible life for sheep — green pastures and still waters in a place where water is chronically scarce. Protection and safety, goodness and mercy are what the good shepherd offers. And so that you and I may experience his fulfilled living, Jesus is prepared to suffer and to die. The love of the shepherd for the sheep costs him his life. He dies not through some accident or the ghastly deed of an uncontrolled mob, but by his willingness to lay down his life. Somehow by his dying on the cross and his rising again there is opened up to me his kind of life. St Paul speaks of it as the mystery. It is given when sin and self are overcome and man is reconciled to his God.

Very clearly, here, Jesus tells us that he is in control and that for this very purpose he was born into the world. So he died for me and for you and for every living creature, that all men and women might have fulfilled lives. Jesus took the total burden of man — his sin, his loneliness, his hunger, his slavery, his disappointment, and his despair — he took it all with him to the cross.

It is at the cross, then, that we meet the Christ. At this place I bring my need, and he brings his saving love, and there is a new beginning.

For reflection

There is a reluctance on our part to meet Christ at the cross. We do not find it easy to bring our need to meet his love. Why is this so?

3 Friday

John 10:19–30

The Jewish people had, and still have, a great sense of history. The feast of the Dedication (v. 22) was an annual event commemorating the restoration of the temple from the desecration at pagan hands, and a renewal of faith. They cherished an image of the Messiah as one who would come and vindicate their cause, who would give them reason for pride, who would make their name great. When they looked at Christ and listened to him they saw him in terms of this image. Thank God that he does not work to our specifications but sends his Son according to his own plan.

Christ is not a projection of what we think of God. Christ is the image that God would give us of himself (2 Cor 4:6). Beware lest we try to fit God into our mould. To make God in our image prevents him from making us in his image. The end result is that we fail to see ourselves as we really are. And we fail to see God's revelation of himself in Christ. We are blind in two ways.

Notice how the Jewish authorities react in this passage. They keep trying to find out what has already been revealed. They are blind to the fact that they are like sheep without a shepherd. And because of this they fail to acknowledge the Good Shepherd as theirs. They know nothing of hearing the voice of the shepherd, or being called by name, or of the miracle of being forgiven in Christ.

We forget how revolutionary and novel is the concept of a God who cares, who weeps, who is troubled and deeply moved by the agony of the world. The Greek could not think of God as one touched by our grief and our sorrow and our infirmities. This seemed sheer nonsense. The stoic believed that all was determined and the course set for us by blind fate. There is nothing we can do about it. The secularist is convinced that there is no one else but ourselves and we are on our own.

But the person in Christ looks to Jesus who is closer than breathing, nearer than hands and feet. Our Lord is one who, when he saw the crowd, had compassion. He was moved to the very depth of his being. That is the same Lord who walks with us today, identifying with our hurts and set-backs and pain and disappointment and death. Let this day be his day, and allow him to share your experience, whether it be joy or sorrow.

For reflection

What do you find helps you to sense the presence of God?

4 Saturday

John 10:31–42

We stand amazed here as we see what is happening. Here are people of God who have been praying and waiting for God to act on their behalf, to restore Israel and vindicate his cause. They anticipate it happening one way. But God does it another. He visits the earth in purity and love and grace. When the people see this, they deliberately pick up stones to kill him. Holiness is not on their agenda. Reconciliation is not what they are looking for. If God is not going to fulfil their desires, then away with God.

None of the devastating logic that Jesus uses has any effect. His final word is an appeal to what they have seen him do: "If you cannot accept my words, then accept my deeds." Everything that Jesus says is supported by what he is and does. His teaching is thoroughly consistent with his life.

Would that this could be said of those who have heard the name of Christ! They not only heard about goodness and righteousness. They saw it in the flesh. They not only heard about love and compassion. They saw it incarnate in Christ. They not only heard about the joy of the kingdom of God. They saw joy in everything that Jesus did. And yet they plotted his death. "Stone him, crucify him" — any way to get rid of him. No act of power or miracle will stir the heart of the person who does not want to believe.

How thankful we should be this day for verses 40–42! There are always some who see their need in the light of his love and are prepared to trust him. Down through the years there have been the small handful who hear his word and reach out for saving. We think of the encouragement those few must have been to the Lord Christ.

Consider, then, what you will be doing this day. Your work takes you into a world that has little room for Jesus Christ. There will be some who may show real enmity against God and against his Son. But most will simply act out the events of the day as though he did not exist. And maybe life has been a disappointment and a burden to some you will meet.

But there will be a few who will encourage the heart of the Master. There will be some who enter the market-place trusting him and looking for his hand of blessing. They will be hearing the hurt and recognizing the cry, and will be ready to reach out in compassion. Will you be one of them?

For reflection

Are you aware not only of what Christ said and did, but of his activity in your life today?

5 Sunday (Lent 1)

John 11:1–16

The gospel of John records only seven of the many miracles or signs that Jesus performed. The writer would have heard about the others many times. But carefully he chooses seven to form a sort of picture gallery of our Lord at work. Each picture shows him meeting a different need and bringing wholeness to the brokenness of life. Let us look at all seven briefly and see how beautifully Jesus ministers to the needs of people.

There is the turning of water into wine (ch 2).
There is the healing of the nobleman's son (4:46).
There is the healing of the man at the pool (ch 5).
There is the feeding of the 5,000 (ch 6).
Christ walks on the water and stills the storm (6:16).
We read of his giving sight to the man born blind (ch 9).

And today we read the seventh miracle, the raising of Lazarus from the dead. Of all human problems death seems to be the greatest. Death is our enemy. The secular mind does not know how to deal with the subject and generally refuses to mention it. The stoical mind accepts it with resignation but sees no meaning in it. Here is the problem. Death is irrevocable, it is final, it is inescapable.

Gratefully, then, we see Christ coming face to face with the grim ogre of death. It is placed beautifully here in a home setting. There is the sudden illness, the resulting anxiety, the decision to summon Jesus, the asking him to hurry before it is too late, and then Jesus' response (v. 4). Until this moment the ultimate tragedy was sickness leading to death. "Not any longer," says Christ. "The destructive sting of death is to be removed. God will be glorified and man blessed." It is a major breakthrough in man's experience with God. For the person in Christ it is now possible for affection, suffering, and even death to be positive, creative, redemptive, and to the glory of God. This is why Jesus did not panic or even hurry to Lazarus's sick bed (v. 6). Our Lord is in complete control, even over death. He is fulfilling his purpose. Blessing and joy come out of the crisis.

This is the way God intends life to be. He invites us to entrust each day the anxiety, the sudden reversal, the doctor's appointment into his loving hands. As in the case of Lazarus he may not move or appear to move immediately. He may delay, bringing strain to our faith and our patience. But if Christ is given his way, God will be glorified and you and I will be blessed.

For reflection

What is your experience of being impatient with God and wondering why he does not reveal himself? Is there a lesson to be learned when our prayers are not quickly answered?

6 *Monday*

John 11:17–27

Is it not extraordinary that this stunning miracle should be recorded only in John's gospel? Is it because Simon Peter is not present through chapters 7–11? Something had kept him at home in Galilee, and therefore he never witnessed this event. Consequently he never passed it on to Luke. It has also been suggested that because Lazarus's life was in danger following his resurrection (12:10) he went into hiding and was not heard of again.

And now we find ourselves present at the scene of family grief. Helplessness and hopelessness are indicated by everything that is said here. And most clearly are they revealed in the scolding words of Martha (11:20–22). This statement of Martha's sums up the cry of agony of a suffering world. Why did my beloved have to die? What is God doing? Why does he allow such suffering? With his resources and his power I would plan it so differently. It is all so unjust. If God be God, how can he be good? There are a thousand ways of asking the same question, and Martha, blinded by disappointment and grief, complains bitterly.

How patient and understanding is Jesus as he replies! He sees the solution to this age-old problem of suffering. It lies in Christ, the resurrection and the life. If you believe that Jesus is alive, then you too have the clue to the great problem. Wherever his abundant life is at work, there is no death, and the believer, though he were dead, yet shall he live. And even as Jesus in infinite love and power turns this scene of grief and disappointment around, and brings life and hope and redemption, so we are called upon with Martha to trust Christ and commit to him the things that happen to us.

Are you faced with illness today and praying desperately for healing? Have you an agenda that you expect God to conform to? Then change your prayer, or you will end up scolding God or doubting him or even rejecting him. Trust him to work redemptively through the pain, the anxiety, the disappointment.

The lame man at the gate asked for money, and God gave him the ability to walk. Martha asked for healing, and Christ gave her a brother raised from dead. Paul asked to be delivered from a thorn in the flesh, and God gave him something else. He taught Paul how sufficient is his grace. The greatest truth here is that God is able to turn every pain, every suffering, every disappointment, every setback into cause for rejoicing. But we must trust him to do it his way.

For reflection

People work out their grief and loss in different ways. Some do it in anger. Some show bitter disappointment and even become cynical. Some accept what happens in resignation. What other way is Jesus teaching us in this passage?

7   *Tuesday*

John 11:28–37

I was a very small boy when I learned that John 11:35 was the shortest verse in the Bible. "Jesus wept." It was many years later before I learned *why* Jesus wept. Did he know that he was about to raise Lazarus from the dead? Was he aware at this point that all would turn out well and that there would be joy? Why then did he weep? Not only did he weep, but he was "deeply moved in spirit and troubled" (v 33).

Surely this means that Jesus was identifying with the grief and sorrow and frustration of death. We can only guess what was going through his mind at this time. There was the destructiveness and waste and loss of human life which must have appalled him. There was the fact that, even were he to restore life to the dead man, Lazarus would have to die again, and that Jesus was simply delaying a problem that would have to be faced another time. There was the cry of agony rising from a world of pain and grief which must have overwhelmed him. There was the possibility that, if death were to be conquered finally, it would involve nothing less than his own death at the hands of sinful man. Somewhere here lies the reason for his being deeply moved in spirit and troubled.

Mary and Martha felt pain and grief at the loss of their brother. It would affect their world. It would seriously disturb their way of life. It would separate them from a loved one. But Jesus sees the larger issue and looks at Lazarus's death as an example of human suffering. It is this larger view that enables Christ to act differently on different occasions. We might call him inconsistent. Here it is recorded that some of them said about Jesus, "Could not he who opened the eyes of the blind man have kept this man from dying?" They sense a kind of inconsistency about Christ. But Christ has his eye on the larger scene.

Surely our prayer today must be that our vision be enlarged. We are prone to view every event of life in terms of its effect upon us. We lose a loved one and are wrapped up in our grief. We sustain an injury or suffer a sickness and think of it in terms of time lost or opportunities missed. We see one person recover and another's condition worsen. We see signs of healing here and none there. And we wonder whether God is even handed.

It will help us to recall this scene of Jesus weeping in frustration and even anger at the forces at work about us. And then, in his own way and in his own time, life appears out of death.

For reflection

What does this passage tell you about answered or unanswered prayer?

8 Wednesday
John 11:38–44

Only three people are recorded in the gospels as having been raised from the dead by the command of Jesus: the widow's son at Nain (Lk 7:11), Jairus's daughter (Lk 8:41), and Lazarus (Jn 11:38). In each case the dead person was restored to vigorous life and the home was filled with rejoicing. The evidence of healthy life appears in the widow's son when he opens his mouth and speaks. The evidence of healthy life in Jairus's daughter appears when Jesus observes that she is hungry and orders food for her. And now, as Lazarus steps out from his grave, Jesus says to those about, "Loose him and let him go."

Surely there are signs here of the quality of life that comes from Jesus. One evidence of new life in Christ is that the mouth is opened and the reborn person is impelled to speak of his new-found faith in his new-found Lord. "We cannot but speak of what we have seen and heard" (Acts 4:20) say Peter and John. And down through the years our experience has been that people of new-found faith in Christ are encouraged to bear public witness to that faith and are able to overcome their reticence.

Our service of Morning Prayer in the *Book of Common Prayer* reminds us of our shortcoming and our unworthiness to approach God. Then we are invited to confess publicly our sin, and the great and comforting absolution is pronounced. It is then that with sin confessed and forgiven we are invited to open our lips so that our mouths may show forth his praise.

Another evidence of new life in Christ is a hunger for the things of God, a hunger that needs to be fed by the word of God. Many times it has been my experience to see new life in Christ followed by an insatiable appetite to know the plan of

God in scripture. Psalm 1 speaks about the happy man delighting in the law of the Lord and meditating in that law day and night.

Yet another evidence of new life in Christ is a sense of being set free. Jesus said, "If the Son makes you free, you will be free indeed" (8:36). A large part of our growing in Christ is understanding what it means to be loosed and set free.

> He breaks the power of cancelled sin,
> He sets the prisoner free.
>
> *Charles Wesley*

In every part of the world, in every language, amidst every culture there are people finding Christ and affirming that they have begun to find real freedom. Secular society believes that money sets one free — or leisure time, or sensual pleasure — until disillusionment sets in. It is Christ who demonstrates in our lives that we can indeed be set free from self. For in allowing him the central place we find a new priority for our time and energy and possessions. There is also the bondage of fear and anxiety. Many things threaten our future. A sick economy, our increasing pollution of air and water, terrorism and the collapse of law and order, starvation and unrest. And fear is a very real experience for many people. Christ can set us free from this bondage.

For reflection

Can you find signs of new life in your relationship with God? Is there some boldness to speak, some hunger for the Word, some sense of new freedom?

9 *Thursday*

John 11:45–53

What had Jesus done? He had raised Lazarus from death. He had shown miraculous power. He had brought joy to the house of Martha and Mary. This was the purpose of Jesus for that home, even before Lazarus died. Jesus is the resurrection and the life. It is his purpose to bring life out of death, and joy out of loss and sorrow and tragedy.

The moment that Saul of Tarsus gave Jesus any opportunity at all, miracle and life-giving power began to be demonstrated. This is the story of the acts of the apostles. Healing of body, new direction to living, prisoners set free, sight given to the blind. The church by these signs shows itself to be the body of Christ. Truly, as the Father had sent the Son, so now the Son is sending the church (20:21).

God's purpose for his people is unchanged. It is to be the church in a world of death and sorrow. The church is called to be a demonstration of miracle and power. It is new life in the Spirit. It is a dead marriage restored to life. It is a home broken by mistrust and silence, and rebuilt around forgiveness and love. The church is God's continuing revelation of himself to the world. It is not individual Christians, each on their own, demonstrating Christ. It is the corporate body of believers breaking bread together in love and then living out the miracle in the world.

The question we now ask is, What affect will this have? Will it work? Have we any hope or confidence that the dying, sorrowing world will respond? This passage reveals the three responses of the secular and unbelieving world to the demonstration of God's miracle.

(v 45) Many saw Lazarus come alive and believed. It is beautiful to see this happen. People ever since have been turning to Christ and finding new life and hope.

(v 46) Some had very real doubts about Jesus. They felt no compelling need for a change in the direction of their lives, and they found Christ's claims for himself and on them disturbing. They wished that he would be quiet, and this has always been so. People left the church because of the claims of Christ. They did not want to hear about surrendering their lives to him.

(v 53) And then there were those who plotted Christ's death (19:8-10) and Lazarus's also. If they could remove the evidence of the life-giving power of Christ, they would stop the growth of the kingdom.

So the church has attracted new believers when Christ has been exalted. So the church has raised doubts in people's minds. So the church has invited persecution and endured much suffering. Such is the response to the life-giving Christ today. Let us pray that we may see the miracle of new life this day in our own lives and in the lives of others.

For reflection

In what ways do you see your parish church as God's continuing revelation of himself to the world?

10 Friday

John 11:54–57

What a marvellous scene! The name of Jesus is on every lip. Some who were captured by his love longed to see him again. But he disappeared (v 54). Others were saying, "Who is this Jesus?" It is the ultimate question. It will not leave us alone. As people prepared for the great festival of the Passover, certain other questions entered their minds. Will the Messiah, the great deliverer, come soon as the scholars predicted? Will the Messiah come at the celebration of the Passover? This was the moment in history when God delivered his people from the hand of the oppressor (Exodus). They have been celebrating the event faithfully ever since. And scholars predicted that God would choose Passover time to deliver his people once again. Will Jesus appear at the Passover? Could they expect him to declare himself with power at this time?

It was an exciting time. They could see him marching in and taking hold and driving out the Romans and freeing the land and the people. So, they thought, he would declare himself. But Jesus had already declared himself in raising Lazarus to new life. His power is not in the march of armies or the clash of weapons but in new life. "If any man be in Christ Jesus, he is a new creation."

His purpose is not to restore kingdoms but to restore the lost image, so that man might become what he was intended to be (Col 3:10). The first chapter of Genesis sees God at work in creation. And the highlight of that creation comes in Genesis 1:26 when he says, "Let us make man in our own image." Volumes have been written attempting to explain the image of God. What was it in man that made him particularly God-like? And what happened to deface that image? Perhaps it is helpful to be reminded that no one has seen God at any time, but the only-begotten of the Father, he has declared him (1:18). So it is that Christ's purpose is to restore in humanity the original image. The self-centred person defaces the image of God. But the new person in Christ begins to be made in his image and someday will be like him (1 Jn 3:2).

So Jesus does arrive in Jerusalem at Passover time. He is about to lead his people once again out of bondage and into the land of promise. But this time it is bondage of sin and self-will that concerns him. Now he attacks the kingdom of broken relationships and mistrust, of injustice and intolerance, of poverty and longing. It is a new kingdom to which he leads his people, and the marks of the kingdom are joy and peace and love.

But it will be a costly victory. There will be no cheap way of bridging the gap between humanity and God, and bringing reconciliation. Nothing short of the giving of himself will do, and the shadow of the cross looms up in these passages.

For reflection

If restoring the lost image in man meant the cross for Christ, in what way does it mean the cross for us?

11 Saturday

John 12:1-8

If you piece together the three pictures recorded about Mary the sister of Martha and Lazarus, you find a woman whose life the Lord has touched. Luke 10:38-41 shows Mary sitting at Jesus' feet listening to everything he has to say to her. In John 11:32 we find Mary again at the feet of Jesus. This time it is an act of worship and devotion. The Lord is about to touch her life again and to bring life into a home saddened by death.

And now in John 12 we find Mary again at Jesus' feet in an extravagant expression of gratitude. The Lord has touched her life, and she must respond. Without counting the cost (about a year's salary) Mary takes the ointment, which is normally measured out in drops, and recklessly pours it all over the feet of her Lord. It was a crazy thing to do. Judas deplores the waste of it all. His relationship with Christ seems to be a calculated one, and in John 17:12 Christ refers to Judas as the son of perdition or the son of wastefulness.

The aristocracy of England called Hudson Taylor's decision to preach Christ in China a shocking waste. His was such a brilliant academic career and his gifts of leadership gave such promise. But Hudson Taylor heard the call of God above the plaudits of the crowd and knew that he must go to China. And his extravagant giving of himself led to the founding of the world's greatest missionary society. Jesus, of course, sees Mary's gift as an act of pure devotion and is encouraged by it. "It will never be forgotten," he says. And raising the whole act to a height Mary never anticipated, Jesus suggests that the ointment is a preparation for his own death and burial.

How little we know or realize when we respond in gratitude to the love of Christ. Most of the stories in the gospels tell of

Christ's love and compassion and grace to those who came to him in need. But this story tells of blessing returned. Jesus blesses the life of Mary, and Mary responds in blessing him. And Jesus takes the responsive act and blesses it in turn.

Such are the dynamics of our relationship with Christ. He blesses our lives by his death and resurrection. He blesses us by giving himself through the sacrament of bread and wine. We respond by offering and presenting ourselves, our souls and bodies to be a reasonable, holy, and living sacrifice. And we leave the service and go out into the world knowing that we are loved and accepted. We are healed and blessed and made whole.

The world calls it a waste of time. Jesus says, "Leave her alone. This is a good thing she is doing." Surely to respond to the love of Christ and give of ourselves is an eternal act, giving new dimension and meaning to all of life as we know it.

For reflection

Could we be accused of giving extravagantly to the Lord's work? Or do we measure our givings and calculate them so that they are of little cost?

12 Sunday (Lent 2)

John 9–19

There is great drama in the passage today. St Luke tells us how the colt was secured (19:28–34). Someone's life has been touched by the power and love of Christ. Was it a son cured? Was it some hidden grief softened? Was it a sin forgiven? We do not know. But in gratitude the healed man assured Christ that, if there is anything he can ever do in the way of service, Jesus has only to ask. So it is that disciples commandeer the colt and, when challenged, simply reply, "The Lord needs it." This is reason enough, and Jesus has what he needs.

In the Eucharist we express our thankfulness by offering our souls and bodies — all that we have, anything that Jesus needs — to be a reasonable, holy, and living sacrifice. What might the Lord need that we have to offer? Our time, our energy, our gift, our money. It may well be that this very day we may be asked to respond to the words, "The Lord needs it."

So begins the triumphal procession, and we are told vividly of the reaction of the crowd. Notice how they regard life in material or "horizontal" terms. There is tremendous excitement among the crowd. In the first place it is Passover time — when they remembered their deliverance out of the hands of the Egyptians. All their hopes and aspirations for deliverance from Rome were revived. Furthermore, the city is swollen with pilgrims who have come from far and wide for the great festival. It was generally believed that if and when God provided deliverance, it would be at such a time.

And then there is the remarkable miracle of the raising of Lazarus. Everyone is talking about it (vv 17, 18). They are expectant. Jesus obviously has the power to act, and now there is the sign of his riding into Jerusalem. The scene is explosive.

The crowd regards it all in horizontal terms. When will we be delivered from the hated enemy? When will God's people come into their own? How will it affect me?

But real life is also spiritual or "vertical." It is encounter with God who intersects our path and breaks in upon our affairs. The people were prepared to accept Jesus on their terms, which were horizontal. And when they found that the life he offered was firstly vertical, their enthusiasm quickly vanished, and within a few days they delivered Jesus to be crucified.

Real living begins when we come face to face with Jesus Christ. "Behold, our King cometh" is a vertical statement. And as we respond we recognize that there are horizontal implications. We will see them in the person who needs compassion, in the sick in hospital, in the lonely and oppressed. Surely we look in and see our need. We look up and recognize the answer to our need in Christ. We look about it and see our ministry.

For reflection

Can you detect times in your own life when Christ is honoured and praised on Sunday, but rejected and even crucified during the week?

13 Monday

John 12:20–26

I will never forget my surprise and exhilaration upon entering a strange pulpit and seeing carved on the desk in front of me "Sir, we would see Jesus." It has been my conviction ever since that the greatest service we can offer our fellow human beings is to introduce them to Jesus Christ. You can imagine the eagerness of Philip and Andrew as they brought these seekers face to face with their Lord and Master.

Remarkable things happen when people see Christ. Simon Peter broke down and wept as he saw Jesus looking at him, and reflected on his denial of Christ. The first disciples, when they saw Christ on that resurrection day, were filled with joy. And now we watch this encounter between the Greeks and Christ the Lord.

Notice what Jesus says, "You are just in time to see the Son of man glorified." There is a cross reference to Exodus 33:19 where Moses asks God, whom he has never seen, to show him his glory. And God says, "I will make all my goodness pass before you and will proclaim before you my name." Here then is the glory of God. It is the goodness of God, his love, his generosity, his long-suffering, his patience. It is seen most clearly as Jesus offers himself for us on the cross and provides reconciliation between God and us.

Here then is the secret of really seeing Jesus. Like a grain of wheat which must go into the ground and die, so we must see Christ at the place where he gives up his life. We look at his life, we look at his teachings, we look at his mighty works, we look at his love. But if we really want to know who he is, we must regard the significance of the cross. To see Jesus is also the secret of belonging. A grain of wheat, if left alone, abides alone. Kernels of wheat were found in King Tutankhamen's tomb 5,000 years after they were placed there, exactly as they were. A few of them were taken and planted, buried in the ground, and they produced fruit.

Aloneness and separation are the problem of modern humanity. We have little or no identity. We are a social security number. We have little sense of belonging. But if we are buried with Christ, if we die to sin and self, we find ourselves being at one with God and part of his family. "I will never leave you nor forsake you," said Jesus to his disciples. And so a new sense of belonging is given to us.

To "see" Jesus is also the secret of a fruitful life. If a grain of wheat goes into the ground and dies, it brings forth much fruit. It is a life forgiven and cleansed, and it begins to show the tender shoots of love and joy and peace.

> When I survey the wondrous Cross
> on which the Prince of glory died,
> My richest gain I count but loss,
> and pour contempt on all my pride.
>
> *Isaac Watts*

For reflection

How would you describe "seeing Jesus" to someone who inquired?

14 Tuesday

John 12:27–34

Something of the conflict going on in the heart of Christ is revealed in this passage. God saved us from ever thinking that the way of the cross was easy for Christ. The agony over the shadow of the cross we associate with the Garden of Gethsemane. But it must have been on his heart and in his mind almost constantly as the event of the cross came closer.

"Now is my soul troubled," says Christ. And then, as if talking to himself, he says, "Shall I beg off? Will I try some way other than the cross? Is there an alternative? Can't God devise a better way, a less painful and humiliating way?" These are the questions that come to the mind of Christ, and to any of us when we are called to give ourselves and yield our independence.

Then for Christ the issue becomes clear. What was the purpose of his becoming man and visiting the earth and sharing in our experience? Was it his teaching? Not mainly. Was it his healing? Not predominantly. It was so that he might give up his life. Only through the work of the cross can I know life eternal. So Jesus rejects the possibility of avoiding the cross and gives full assent to the plan when he says, "Father, glorify thy name." Clearly Jesus sees three consequences of his being obedient to the death of the cross.

1   "Now is the judgment of this world" (v 31). Here the destructive enmity in the heart of humanity would confront the healing and life-giving love that is in the heart of God. The cross would become the crisis. It is here at the cross that you and I must make a decision about God and life and ourselves. "This is how the judgment works," says John. "The light has come into the world, but people love the darkness rather than light, because their deeds were evil" (3:19).

2   Now shall the ruler of this world be cast out (v 31). Here at the cross the grip of evil is broken and we are now able to say with Paul, "Sin will have no dominion over you." (Romans 6:14). No longer are we able to say in our sin and failure, "I am only human." Now by the power of the cross we can claim victory over sin and defeat and loneliness.

3   "And I, when I am lifted up from the earth, will draw all men to myself" (v 32). Here is the third consequence of the cross. It will serve as a magnet drawing men and women who long for fulfilment and healing, for forgiveness and grace, to the Lord Jesus Christ. Here we find new life and here we are made new people.

These, then, must have been some of the thoughts that reveal the conflict in the mind of Christ. With great love and resolute purpose he saw the issues clearly and offered himself for our salvation.

Were the whole realm of nature mine,
That were an offering far too small;
Love so amazing, so divine,
Demands my life, my soul, my all.

Isaac Watts

For reflection

It is easy to wear the cross. It is another thing to bear the cross.

15 Wednesday

John 12:35–43

The remaining part of the twelfth chapter of John is full of peri-
lous possibilities. There are three distinct warnings given by
our Lord as he addresses himself to the many different kinds of
people facing him. He knows who are the hungry of heart and
the responsive. He also knows who are hostile to him and,
even more important, those who are neutral and uncommit-
ted. We will deal with the first two warnings in the chapter.

The first comes in verse 35: "Walk while you have the light,
lest the darkness overtake you." I wonder if Jesus at this point
was appalled at the lack of response from the people. They had
heard him teach. They had seen Lazarus raised from the dead.
They were witnesses to the Master's grace and love. They were
bathed in the light. But, as John says (3:19), "This is the judgment, that the light has come into the world, and men loved
darkness rather than light, because their deeds were evil."

How long do you expect this light to last? How long do you
expect to be able to see and hear God's incarnation of himself?
Not forever; that is certain. There is a limited time. And surely
Christ was referring to his ministry. His earthly ministry was
just a brief flash of light in the dark gloom of history. We see
him hiding himself from the curious public. We see him giving
his last word to the unresponsive people. We see him after his
resurrection appearing only to those who wanted him. And
then they saw him no more. That opportunity had passed.

But there is a wide application here in the area of human
experience. Surely the decision to trust Christ must be made in
time. "Now is the acceptable time; behold, now is the day of
salvation" (2 Cor 6:2). Surely the opportunities that are ours in
word and sacrament, in church and fellowship, in freedom of

conscience and freedom to assemble and worship must not be taken for granted. The impact of the word of God on our ears and hearts is dynamic. We cannot continue hearing without some response, some melting of the heart, some yielding of the will. Otherwise our response mechanism will be damaged and our will to choose lessened. Blindness sets in when the light is shut out. Closed eyes and closed hearts become blinded eyes and hardened hearts. Here then is Christ's first warning.

The second warning concerns what happens when we love the praise of other people more than the praise of God (v 43). We can all identify with this danger. How often we have remained silent, fearing the displeasure of our peers, rather than speaking out against injustice or prejudice or obvious evil. We live in the middle of situations that cannot be pleasing to God. Are we ready to raise our voices and risk the displeasure of our friends who have vested interests?

> God send us men with hearts ablaze
> All truth to love, all wrong to hate;
> These are the patriots nations need,
> These are the bulwarks of the State.
>
> *Frederick John Gillman*

For reflection

Do we remember to pray for Christians living in the middle of oppression and injustice, that they may have courage and wisdom?

16 Thursday

John 12:44–50

Here is the third in a series of three warnings uttered by our Lord. The first (12:35) is that opportunities for belief are not limited. The second warning (12:43) is that the praise of men can appear to be more attractive than the praise of God.

The third warning concerns the certainty of judgment (v 49), a concept almost universally misunderstood. Vaguely lurking in the back of our minds is the fear that somehow God will punish us for our misdoings. People cling to a ledger theology, which balances good against evil and hopes that the balance will be favourable when the final tally is made. This concept of judgment is human and does not come from scripture. The passage makes it very clear that God does not judge in this way, but brings all things to the light. "God is light and in him is no darkness at all" (1 Jn 1:5).

Improve the lighting anywhere, and hidden dirt and shabbiness will be revealed. Shine a flashlight into a corner of a seldom used cellar, and crawlers will scurry for cover. Allow the light of Jesus Christ to penetrate any section of life or society, and the ugliness of human nature — its greed, its self-centredness — will very quickly appear.

You can see this happening as Jesus encountered self-satisfied people. Zaccheus (Lk 19:1–10) was delighted to have Jesus come to his home. But when Jesus visited him, the light of his love and grace penetrated the dark corners of that man's life and home, and Zaccheus became aware for the first time how shabby his life was and how tawdry his possessions. What he considered before as clever acquisitions, gained by outsmarting and cheating the poor, now were viewed as sordid and unworthy. Zaccheus could not get rid of them quickly enough.

This is the judgment that surely comes upon us as we encounter Christ and hear his word. It is Christ's longing for us that our lives, our relationships, our business dealings, our private thoughts, our reading, all be opened up to the light so that we can see it for what it is. And then we cry for cleansing and renewal.

Such was the experience of a young man who came into the light of Jesus Christ. Before this experience he had cleverly pilfered from the company's till and supply store room. He considered it clever and prided himself in not being discovered. But Jesus Christ touched his life, and he saw it all under the illuminating gaze of the Son of God. He came under judgment and was moved to confess the situation to his superior and risk dismissal from his job.

Such is the light of Christ coming into our lives. He illuminates. But he also brings warmth and healing and new life and growth. Our prayer book Eucharist introduces us to a God "unto whom all hearts are open, all desires known, and from whom no secrets are hid." Only when we come under the searchlight of his gaze can we truly confess our sin and receive his absolution. Here is the source of joy and thanksgiving.

For reflection

Read John 3:19 on the subject of judgment.

17 Friday

John 13:1–11

This story of Jesus washing the disciples' feet appears often in stained glass. It is a story much loved, and it is often sentimentalized so that its real meaning may be lost. We like to act out the story on Maundy Thursday, carefully choosing someone whose feet do not need washing and going through the charade with silver bowl and fine linen.

This feet washing is filled with surprise; it is disturbing. It cuts through all we understand about dignity and position and rights and proper pecking order. The disciples were preoccupied with this question. They were busy getting this order straight (Lk 22:24). Jesus would be first, of course; then it would be Andrew, or maybe Peter. It would depend on how one makes the judgment. This is the natural approach to the whole matter. The senior executive has the private washroom and the office with the best view. The junior executives have to share and do not have wall to wall carpeting. We understand this. How else would it be?

It is when we ask this question that Jesus shows us his order of preference. He reversed the accepted order of things. He exposed the disciples as people who were committed to worldly judgment. He gave to them and to us a picture of God that is quite unacceptable. Every person in that upper room would have been quite willing and even eager to wash Jesus' feet. This would be right and proper by human standards. We are ready to humble ourselves before God, but we don't want him humbling himself before us. We want our God to be a great God — mighty and loving. We want to be distinguished by our God.

Imagine, then, the complete surprise of the twelve when Jesus reverses the accepted order of things and does the unthinkable. The Lord God becomes the servant. When they object, he insists. This is the basis on which the new relationship between God and humanity is founded. We must first of all allow God to minister to our deep need. "If I do not wash you, you have no part in me" (v 8). He must be allowed to forgive and to bless. And we must in humbleness acknowledge our need and be open to his blessing.

Consider Jesus' love shining through all he knew. He knew that his hour had come, with all its agony and desolation. This would be enough to absorb our every thought. He knew that Judas Iscariot was about to betray him. Yet he thought only of his beloved twelve and longed for them to realize all the possibilities of this hour. Let us reflect this day on that unfailing love which gives of himself, and gives and gives again. And then, as he longs for response from us, he says, "Give me your heart."

For reflection

Can you suggest some action today which could be considered a modern counterpart of "feet washing?"

18 Saturday

John 13:12–20

The disciples are still reeling from the surprise of having their feet washed by the Master when the second surprise is put before them. Once again they are caught off balance. It has been made clear that they must allow the Saviour to be the servant and minister to their need. Now Jesus tells them that they must be ready to do this for each other. "You also ought to wash one another's feet."

In a world where greatness and success were judged by the number of your servants, it would take a whole new mind set to grasp a totally different standard of greatness. Frequent references appear in the gospels to disagreements and arguments among the disciples about who would be greatest in the kingdom (Lk 22:24–27). We should read Christ's answer to the questions raised there. Men and women who are in Christ are introduced to a new ministry. It is a ministry to people. It is a deep concern for other people's needs. It is a willingness to forego rights and privileges and to do the work of a servant.

Washing of feet really has no meaning in our society. We have to find out with loving concern where the need is and address ourselves to it. This begins with our overcoming the human desire to put self first. It comes when we refuse to say, "That's his problem," and begin to accept it as ours. Human nature is enormously absorbed in itself. The new nature that Christ gives is listening to what others are saying, it is feeling the hurt, it is sharing the bread, it is opening the home and the heart, it is showing compassion, it is recognizing injustice and speaking out on behalf of the oppressed. This is what Christ meant when he suggested that we wash one another's feet.

Today we will pick up the paper or turn on the television set, and we will be battered with suffering and hunger and pain. The weight of the world's problems is overwhelming. We cannot absorb any more, and we are filled with frustration. The great danger is that we might lose our compassion and concern ourselves with our own problems. But Jesus, knowing who he was, knowing the immanence of the cross, knowing that Judas was about to betray him, knowing the hearts of each one of us, took a towel and a basin of water and washed the disciples' feet. And then he directed them to wash each other's feet.

Here then is the answer Christ would give us to the world's pain. Be ready to minister this very day to someone you encounter. Be listening for the cry for help, and enter into the compassion of Jesus. This will not come to us naturally. This is the gift of God. We must ask him for it. "If you know these things, blessed are you if you do them."

For reflection

Lord of all kindliness, Lord of all grace,
Your hands swift to welcome, your arms to embrace,
Be there at our homing, and give us, we pray,
Your love in our hearts, Lord, at the eve of the day.

Jan Struther

19   Sunday (Lent 3)

John 13:21–30

It is well said that the sun that melts the butter hardens the clay. Simon Peter must have been moved to tears as Jesus took his feet in his hands and washed them. Would he ever forget that moment? Years later in writing his first epistle, he speaks of girding oneself with the towel of humility (1 Pet 5:5), and surely it was the scene in the upper room that he had in mind.

But Judas seems to have gone through the same experience unmoved. We might well ask how he could do it. How would he hear those words of the Lord, "One of you will betray me?" How could he accept the morsel from Jesus signifying love and trust and friendship? How could he hear Jesus say, "What you are about to do, do quickly," and immediately leave the room knowing that Jesus' eyes followed him with pain right to the door? Indeed it was night (v 30). It was one of the darkest moments in the experience of man and is remembered with horror even to this day.

Why did it have to be? Jesus is generous in giving Judas opportunities to back out and save the situation. But Judas seems hell-bent at this moment. When Jesus was choosing the twelve, did he not see Judas as susceptible to thievery and betrayal? Were there tell-tale signs along the way that might have warned Jesus? Indeed there were. Jesus alludes to Judas as the son of perdition (17:12). Is Judas bound to be lost so that the scripture might come true? We reject the implication here that Jesus chose Judas because the prophet of old called for a betrayer.

It was Palm Sunday evening and the group of college students had gathered after Evensong for questions and discussion. The visiting preacher had chosen Judas for his sermon subject, and our thoughts were on him. A question was raised by one of the students. If the prophecy called for a betrayal and Judas had not done it, who would have done it? There was a long pause, and then the visitor replied to the student, "I believe I would have done it."

Certainly Judas must have been as promising a disciple as any of the others. Jesus was drawn to his enthusiasm and recognized his gifts and wanted him on the team. Anyone of the twelve could have been the betrayer. Peter was the one who openly denied Christ. But they all forsook him and fled.

This day you may find yourself at the point of betrayal. You could be the enemy of Christ by your silence when something needs to be said for Christ, by your reaction to some remark, by your consent to dishonesty. Even as Christ chose Judas knowing that he was capable of betrayal, so he has chosen us knowing our weakness and our self-centredness. But he loves us to the end, and is always ready to restore and to forgive.

For reflection

When Jesus called you because he loves you by way of baptism and commitment and heart response, he did so knowing your strengths and your weaknesses. What sort of risk have you proved to be?

20 *Monday*

John 13:31–38

Do we sense a relief of tension now that Judas has left the room? Jesus must feel freer to talk now. He has so much to tell them. We might perhaps expect some comment about the betrayer who has left the gathering. But no, there is no resentment, no recrimination, just sorrow that this should happen to one of the inner circle.

"Now is the Son of man glorified," says Christ. What is the glory of God? What are we to look for in Jesus as a glorified person? In Exodus 33 we have an encounter between Moses and the Lord. It says that the Lord would speak to Moses face to face as a man speaks to his friend (Ex 33:11). In this conversation Moses asks for some indication of God's plan for the future. Moses seeks some affirmation of God's promise and asks God to show him his glory (Ex 33:18). The Lord's reply to that request (v 19) is, "I will make all my goodness pass before you."

This is what we are to understand about the glory of God. It is the character of God, the goodness of God, the love and compassion of God revealed in and through his Son. Jesus is saying (v 31) that the character of God is about to be revealed in a new and startling way. It will be revealed most splendidly at the cross. If you want to know what God is really like, you √ must go to the cross and see him pouring out his life for the sin of the world. It is the supreme act of love.

Most of us will know some lovely, gentle people who call themselves agnostic. They believe in some sort of impersonal God, but they maintain that you cannot know him. But scripture states very clearly that God has made himself known and we meet him where his character is declared. We meet him at the place of repentance and faith. "God was in Christ; reconciling the world unto himself" (2 Cor 5:19). Here is God glorified. And he is also glorified and his character revealed as those who acknowledge him as Lord and Saviour love one another. The commandment to love one another really summarizes all that God would have us be and do. He wants us to be a reflection of himself.

Our immediate reaction is to say that we can do this in our own strength. Simon Peter argues vehemently that he is capable of such love and loyalty (v 37). But Jesus knows better and warns him of failure ahead. There is too much of self in Simon Peter for this response of love. In the same way we cannot respond to God's love or love one another until the self is dealt with. Only the Spirit of God can do this.

For reflection

Spirit of God, descend upon my heart;
Wean it from earth; through all its pulses move;
Stoop to my weakness, mighty as thou art,
And make me love thee as I ought to love.

George Croly

21   Tuesday

John 14:1-7

I wonder whether a long silence does not occur at the end of chapter 13. Simon Peter is so sure and outspoken as he vows loyalty to Christ, and then he is stunned by Jesus' prophetic words (13:38): "Will you lay down your life for me? Truly, truly, I say to you, the cock will not crow, till you have denied me three times." How little we know about ourselves! Simon Peter cannot believe what Jesus has just said about him. Does he go into an uncharacteristic period of silence? And does Jesus address those first words of chapter 14 to Simon Peter? "Let not your hearts be troubled." Ahead may be denial and failure and lack of trust. But ahead lies also forgiveness and restoration and renewal of trust in the power and the promise of God. Jesus takes the uncertainty and the anxiety out of the future.

In the first place, he has gone ahead. He has shared our experience of life to the full and suffered death and piloted the way for us from temporal life to eternal life. The writer of the letter to the Hebrews speaks of Jesus as a forerunner on our behalf (Heb 6:19) who has entered into the inner shrine behind the curtain. St Paul recognized that Jesus has conquered the future and taken the sting out of death (1 Cor 15:55). So our burial service, while recognizing grief and loss, is filled with joy and expectancy.

In the second place, Jesus has prepared a place for us. Many attempts have been made to explain what Jesus meant by many mansions or many rooms. Someone has suggested that the way ahead is a long, hard pilgrimage but along the way are resting places as one would have on an oriental journey. We can be encouraged in our reading today that, although ahead of us are pitfalls and heartache and weariness, Jesus prepared for us places of refreshment and renewal. Perhaps then we can recognize in word and sacrament, in fellowship and joy, moments when the soul is encouraged and we find the strength to continue.

In the third place, Jesus has removed the anxiety from the future in his promise to return. This was a strong hope in the mind of the early church. Over and over the expectation of Christ's return is underlined. As Jesus disappeared from sight in Acts 1, the word given to the disciples was that "this Jesus, who was taken up from you into heaven, will come in the same way as you saw him go into heaven" (Acts 1:11).

To this glorious end is history moving. When and where and how we do not know. But the believer in Christ is called upon to live each day as though the Lord Jesus would return. This means living one day at a time with a heart forgiven, with relationships healed and with sure purpose. "Wherefore," says St Paul, "comfort one another with these words" (1 Thess 4:18).

For reflection

How does the fact that Jesus suffered shame and pain and death help us in our pilgrimage?

22   *Wednesday*

John 14:8–14

There are three staggering statements in this passage which must have given the disciples much cause for discussion and reflection. These same statements have never ceased to amaze the church to this very day. Let us examine them.

The first surprising statement is in verse 9, where Jesus says to Philip, "He who has seen me has seen the Father." The people of Israel were brought up with the teaching that no one can look upon the face of God and live (Ex 33:20). "No one has ever seen God at any time" says St John. This was perfectly clear to those who longed after God. What they now have to learn is that the only begotten Son of the Father, he hath declared him (1:18). What extraordinary news! No longer need we cry as they did in the Old Testament, "O, that I knew where I might find him" (Job 23:3). Now standing before the disciples Jesus says, "If you have seen me, you have seen God." And lest there be some doubt about this, he invites them and us to examine his words of grace and his works of mercy and love (vv 10–11).

The second surprising statement appears in verse 12, where Jesus stuns the disciples with these words: "He who believes in me will also do the works that I do. Yes, even greater works because I go to the Father." Can this possibly be true? We think of the stilling of the storm and the feeding of the multitude. And we wonder about Jesus' statement in verse 12. There were some great works in the Acts of the Apostles but none greater than Christ's works.

But Jesus connects it all with his going and then the coming of the Holy Spirit. Because of the work of the Spirit, Jesus' limited ministry, confined to a small area, would spread through the whole world. The disciples, who in the gospels were pre-occupied with themselves and ridden with fear, would take on new courage and a boldness to speak out for Christ. And Jesus saw ahead and down through the ages the world missionary movement, the barriers of race and prejudice broken down, and men and women moved by the power of the Spirit to come to Christ. These surely are the greater works.

The third surprising statement is in verse 14. "If you ask anything in my name, I will do it." What a dangerous statement, and how it has been abused! The operative phrase is "in my name," and it clearly indicates that the prayer of the Christian needs to be in tune with the will of God. Personal desires and ambitions are ruled out as we bring our thoughts and aspirations into harmony with his.

A surprising passage indeed! To see Christ is to see God. When the Holy Spirit is allowed to work, great things happen. All prayer that is in harmony with the will of God is answered. These facts could provide for us a surprising day.

For reflection

St Paul writes about being on tiptoe of expectancy (Rom 8:19). What surprise might Christ have in store for you today?

23 Thursday

John 14:15–24

A troubled woman came to me in distress because all her life she had been told to love God, but in actual fact she felt no love for him whatsoever. She was trying to feel love as an emotional experience. She had tried saying "Jesus, I love you, I love you" over and over again, using it as a kind of mantra. But it apparently did nothing for her.

Surely Jesus speaks to her problem in this passage. The way to test one's love for Christ is not measured by emotion or by incantation but by the willingness to obey. We know only too well about people who say they love but who cause the loved one pain and heartache. A husband may say that he loves his wife but prove, in fact, to be inconsiderate and difficult to live with.

Real love is shown in its willingness to surrender to the wishes of the other person. This is what Jesus means when he says, "Do you say that you love me? Then find out what I want for you and do it." Demanding? Yes indeed, and costly. If secular people tend to do what they want whenever they want, reason and experience tell us that they are not going to surrender without a very real struggle. But this is exactly what the Lord asks of us if we commit our lives to him.

This is the struggle we see so clearly depicted in the gospels. The price of real commitment was too high for Judas Iscariot. Obedience to the will of Christ demanded too much of him. It was almost too much for Simon Peter. The others, when faced with the decision, forsook Christ and fled. They wanted to hang loose, enjoying the companionship of Jesus, but were not prepared for the kind of commitment that was asked for.

Is Jesus asking for too much here? Do you suppose that he requires the same demanding response from us? We must remember two great and important principles.

The first is that our membership in the church, our claim to be Christian, our allegiance to the cross of Christ implies a relationship with Jesus Christ. Too much religious activity does not understand this relationship. To surrender to Jesus Christ is a relationship of love and, therefore, it implies a blending of our will with his. To resist this is natural. We want to be free to do as we will. But in doing this we damage the relationship.

The second principle is that, in being asked to surrender our freedom to be ourselves, we discover that the service for Christ becomes perfect freedom and we are delivered from very real bondage.

So Jesus wants the best kind of relationship with us because this is the pathway to wholeness and purpose and fulfilment. As we reflect on these things and see repeated failure, we are surprised by his mercy and his restoring grace.

For reflection

In what ways does a good marriage relationship reflect the relationship between Christ and his Church (Eph 5:25–32)?

24 Friday

John 14:25–31

Gradually and tenderly Jesus now begins to deflect the focus of attention away from his physical presence to the unseen presence of the Holy Spirit. Like a father teaching his child a new skill, like walking or swimming, so Christ must teach the new person in Christ to depend not upon his senses but upon his understanding the unseen. The natural mind wants to see and touch and hear. To learn to depend upon and trust the invisible is an acquired skill and does not come readily. Mary reaches out to touch Jesus (20:17) to convince herself that he is real. Jesus discourages this and points her to a new kind of reality — the reality of the Spirit.

St Paul says, "the things that are seen are transient, but the things that are unseen are eternal" (2 Cor 4:18). We need to remember this as we read the post-resurrection events. Jesus appears and disappears giving convincing proof that his physical presence is not essential now. It is even better if he cannot be seen or touched. The ministry of the Holy Spirit will be more effective and even more real (20:29).

So Jesus promises the Holy Spirit or Comforter, or Strengthener or Advocate or Paraclete. Those words convey many pictures. The law court is seen here with the counsel pleading my cause. The army is here, dispirited and receiving encouragement. The pictures all indicate someone in trouble and the Spirit of God making it possible to cope. Jesus would move the disciples away from sentimental remembrance. We have not a trace of a description of his appearance. His childhood and youth with one exception (Lk 2:41) are blacked out. He bids the disciples to look, not back but forward, to the coming of the Holy Spirit.

Such is our blindness that often we dread most the things that contain the most possibility of blessing. The greatest fear for the disciples was that Jesus might leave them. They could not imagine how they would manage. But Jesus says to them and to us, "Let not your hearts be troubled, neither let them be afraid" (v 27).

What do we dread most? Is it something we see or hear or sense? It may seem real enough, but the reality is that we walk by faith, not by sight. The Holy Spirit is in our midst and waits to fill us. The Holy Spirit will point us consistently to the Lord Christ. The Holy Spirit will teach us all we need to know about God and about ourselves. The Holy Spirit will place the very words of Christ on our hearts. The Holy Spirit will quieten the heart and mind with the very peace of God.

For reflection

Ye fearful saints, fresh courage take;
The clouds ye so much dread
Are big with mercy, and shall break
In blessings on your head.

William Cowper

25 Saturday
John 15:1-11

Chapter 14 concludes with our Lord saying to his disciples in the upper room, "Rise, let us go hence." It has been suggested that they proceeded toward the garden of Gethsemane and on the way they came to the gate of the temple on which the vine was emblazoned. This would suggest to the mind of Christ the words of this passage.

Throughout the pages of the Old Testament the vine is the symbol of Israel (Jer 2:21, Ps 80:8). The symbol was on their coins and in relief on the temple gate. The vine was an appropriate symbol and could be well understood by a vine-growing nation. The vine needs constant attention and irrigation and pruning. The vine has one purpose only; it is useless for timber or shade or even firewood. It has little beauty and virtually no noticeable flower. It grows solely for the purpose of producing fruit. The wine is secured after pressure and crushing.

Now, Israel, symbolized by the vine, was a nation with a God-given purpose. Much attention was given to it by the vine-dresser who dug it and fertilized it and watered it in the expectancy that it would bring forth the fruit of righteousness and love and obedience. But the result was failure (Is 5:1-2), and there is heartache and disappointment.

With this in mind Jesus points to the symbol on the temple gate and says, "I am the vine and you are the branches" (v 5). In a most vivid way Jesus is calling for a new beginning with new shoots and branches drawing their life from him and producing fruit. He is speaking not only to the disciples but to every believer. We are the planting of the Lord. His expectation of us is that we produce fruit. The fruit is not success or a good appearance or good health. The fruit Christ expects of us is what he produced — love, joy, peace. . . (Gal 5:22). He expects us to grow like him.

So it is that we must continue to draw our life from Christ. We must abide in him. We become detached from the indwelling power of Christ and from the fellowship of the church at our own peril. There must be pruning when areas of our life which are non-productive must be cut away and burned. The prime objective is to produce fruit which is Christ-like. Anything less is unproductive and must go. How important, then, it is for us this day to "abide in Christ." Our only hope of bearing fruit is that Christ live within us and show himself through our deeds and words and relationships.

As the lights inside a church illuminate the beautiful windows and show the story on the stained glass for the passerby to see, so Christ would live in us daily and reveal himself in us.

For reflection

Using scriptural standards, how would you describe a productive life?

26 Sunday (Lent 4)

John 15:12–17

It is strange that so many people have dismissed the Christian faith as a set of rules for living. They talk about the "do's" but more about the "don'ts" of the Christian faith. Archie Bunker, in one of the television shows, had a terrible nightmare in which he dreamed that he had "flunked heaven," as he described it. He had apparently been examined according to the code of rules and had not come up to standard.

The fact is that there is really no code of rules and Jesus does not lay down any legislation. Certainly, in subsequent years the church has taken pains to spell out what a Christian should or should not do. And there has been much disagreement between various branches of the church over the rules of conduct. Furthermore, the rules have changed from age to age so that what was forbidden fifty years ago may well be accepted now.

This passage is a great help to us in the whole question of what is right and what is wrong. It is a positive statement about the relationship between Christ and those who trust him as Lord and Saviour. It is a relationship of love which Jesus is looking for. He described it as friendship — a deep lasting friendship where he is prepared to lay down his life for us and we should be prepared to do the same for each other. He commands us to love one another and says that, if we are obedient to that command, we are his friends. It is not based on a servile obedience. It is based on one friend doing what the other one wishes.

How remarkable this is! It lifts the whole Christian faith to a level far above negative rules and moral nit-picking. It recognizes the foundation of the ten commandments, but goes much further when it expects us to love the Lord our God with all our heart and mind and strength and our neighbour as ourselves.

The Lord Jesus speaks to our situation out of this passage. One may keep all the "rules" about alcohol and Sunday observance. But how one treats employees or what one is like to live with may never come to mind. This is the danger of living by rule and not by relationship. To be a friend of God means that your relationships are right. To be a friend of God denies you the right to be racist or to discriminate unjustly against anyone.

This can change your day. If faith in Christ Jesus is for you a deepening friendship with him and with the people you meet, you will find that this must be part of your day. It is not something for Sunday observance and detached from the rest of the week. It means that your stand for Christ will be known by your love for the people you meet today.

For reflection

Our love for God whom we cannot see and for Christ whom having not seen we love, must be proved by our love for those around us whom we *can* see. Just as God loved us without any merit in us, so our love must go out for all for whom Christ died whether we find them attractive or not.

Archbishop William Temple

27 Monday

John 15:18–27

The words in this passage seem very strange indeed. Is it true that the Christian can expect to meet hostility because of his stand for Christ? Where in our country does this happen today?

It certainly was a reality in the early days of the church (Mk 13:9–13), and became a familiar scene in the Acts of the Apostles. They knew what it was to be taken before kings and governors. There was no neutrality in those days. In many places to be a Christian invited persecution and even death. The Christian was accused of being disloyal to Caesar. It was a simple matter for the public in the provincial town far from Rome to acknowledge the lordship of Caesar by placing a pinch of salt on the flame. But the Christian could not do this. To do so would be an acknowledgement that Caesar is Lord. But, for the early Christian, Jesus is Lord. His authority and sovereignty could not be shared. And the Christian suffered the consequences.

The service of Holy Communion was misunderstood, and in eating the body of Christ he was accused of cannibalism. Christians were suspected of immorality because of the kiss of peace. They were accused of disrupting family life because of Jesus' teaching (Matt 10:34). Hostility became very familiar to the early believers. They would remember these words of Jesus, "If they persecuted me, they will persecute you."

But what about today? We know that persecution against the Christian is well authenticated in many parts of the world. But the reproach of Christ is universal, and we should be aware of it and understand it (v 22). The writer to the Hebrews tells of Moses' refusal to enjoy the comforts and privileges of the king's palace and his choice to suffer with God's people. The scorn he suffered bcause of God's program was preferable to all the treasures of Egypt (Heb 11:24–26).

The person who trusts Christ and believes his word will always stand out in the community. In representing Christ one must face questions that others may prefer to avoid. The presence of Christ and the witness to Christ is a disturbing factor in the secular community. The Christian runs against the stream and can well be scorned or hated as a result. This creates difficulties and forces the Christian to make a decision either to run away from the enmity that is in the world and find shelter in one's own ghetto or church, or to move out where the unbeliever lives and trim the disturbing factor in one's witness. The Christian can remove the offence and the reproach. But by doing this one forfeits uniqueness in Christ and one's witness is silenced.

Christ here points to a third way. As Christ loved and lived among people, they were faced with a decision, "Either I must be like him, or he must go." The result was the crucifixion. Even so the Lord Christ expects our witness for him to be both loving and penetrating; both appealing and disturbing. And the result may well produce hostility.

It was the Christian family that greeted the new people on the street. No one else went near them. They would depress the value of the real estate. They were undesirable. They were black. But the people in Christ greeted them and loved them as Christ would do. And the Christians incurred the wrath of the rest of the street.

"If the world hates you, know that it has hated me before it hated you."

For reflection

Can you cite an unpopular stand that a Christian might have to take in today's society?

28   Tuesday

John 16:1–11

Jesus' words were prophetic and help us to understand the meaning of Pentecost and the coming of the Holy Spirit upon the church. The disciples must have thought that he was speaking to them in riddles, but carefully Jesus takes them step by step along the way. He knows only too well their weakness and ours. He knows also how alien are the concepts of the unseen in a world that is guided by sensory perception.

St John gives much space to record Jesus' teaching about the Holy Spirit. This was a critical time in the spiritual development of the disciples. They had known of the God of the Old Testament. He was unseen; he spoke through scripture and history and prophets. But mostly he was silent. They reached out to him longing to know him better. And then Jesus came in the flesh, and they were introduced to God the Son. They began to recognize God's plan for them in Christ as he shared our life, gave himself to the death of the cross, and then triumphed over that death in resurrection. The revelation of God in Christ was a life-transforming experience.

But now there is a new development, something just as unexpected and "other" as was the birth of Christ. God is full of surprises as he deals with us. The beloved Christ whom they had grown to love kept speaking about leaving them. However would they manage? They were powerless without him. They could not grasp what he was saying. "It is to your advantage that I go away" (v 7). Patiently and tenderly he introduces them to the next mighty act of God — the coming of the Holy Spirit. When Jesus disappears from sight and the Holy Spirit comes in power, it will be another step forward in God's revelation of himself. Things will be better. The believer will never be left alone. We will be set free from previous limits of geography and time.

There was a day when Jesus took three of his disciples up a mountain for a time of refreshment and encouragement. The other nine were left to deal with the situation down below (Lk 9:28-37). Jesus could not be in two places at one time. Now a new day is coming and this problem will be overcome. The Holy Spirit will live in the hearts of every believer who is open and receptive. Whether you are in church or in hospital, at work or at home, there is the Spirit of God.

The Spirit convicts men and women of sin. How? By pointing them always to Jesus Christ and calling for some decision. For God to respond to our need and send his Son, and then for people to fail to see his beauty and reject him — surely this is the very epitome of sin. The Spirit will be a convincing proof of righteousness. For the Spirit which governed the life and actions of Jesus, and showed him to be righteous, will also govern the hearts of believers and transform their lives so that all will see God's goodness. And finally, the Spirit will speak of judgment. Whoever trusts Christ is delivered from condemnation and declared free. But whoever stands in judgment will find himself judged and condemned even as they did at Jesus' trial.

"It is going to be better," says Jesus, and subsequent events proved him right. This day the Holy Spirit would dwell within us assuring us of the reality of Jesus and blessing our hearts.

For reflection

God would always be teaching us some new thing about himself. Have you received any new insight recently about the love of God?

29   Wednesday

John 16:12–15

To be agnostic about our God is to contradict all that God is saying to us about himself. He is a communicating God revealing to us all that we can grasp of his nature. God the Son reveals to us the essence of God the Father. "No one has ever seen God. The only Son who is the same as God and is at the Father's side, he has made him known" (1:18 TEV).

But now we find that the Holy Spirit is the agent who will teach us all we need to know. "He will guide you into all the truth" (v 13). What a remarkable statement! There is so much that is hidden from our natural state but that will be revealed to us as we are in Christ. The Holy Spirit illuminates the word of God so that the pages come alive for us.

1   We will learn the eternal plan of God for us. We will be able to see the beginning even to the end and a clear, untangled plan connecting the two. We will observe that we were created in the image of God (Gen 1:26), which means that we were made like Christ who is the very image of God. We will see how that image was defaced by man's self-centredness and man was separated from God. We will see how God reached across the chasm and made atonement for us in Christ so that we might become one with him. And we will see that the believer is now being transformed into the image of Jesus Christ so that when he returns we shall be like him.

2   The Holy Spirit, in guiding us into all truth, will provide for us what we need to know to live today. All about us are shifting and eroding standards of morality. There are groups and cults who are declaring what is right in this confusing day. Who knows what is right? What does God expect of those who are in Christ? Jesus said that the Holy Spirit would guide us

into the truth about these matters. Surely we must claim this promise of scripture and bring vexing problems before him in humility and prayer for clarification. We face subtle forms of injustice and oppression. We encounter racial prejudice and discrimination. We are confused about medical ethics. We question abortion and euthanasia and homosexuality. Let us keep our head; let us not panic. If the Holy Spirit is to guide us into all truth, then in answer to our fervent prayer there should be given some position that is consistent with scripture.

3   Finally, the Holy Spirit will point ahead and give to us a sense of destiny and direction. Our story is not like some detective novel where we do not know how it all turns out until the last page. We know, and the Holy Spirit confirms this, that the future belongs to God. Finally, all things will be in Christ. We are the family of God. We are the people of Jesus Christ. We are born of the Spirit. He is declaring to us what we need to know.

For Reflection

Teach us to know the Father, Son,
and thee, of Both, to be but One;
That through the ages all along
This may be our endless song,
    Praise to thy eternal merit,
    Father, Son, and Holy Spirit.

tr. from Latin by Bishop John Cosin

30 Thursday

John 16:16–24

The key word in this passage is *joy*. It is a word which more often than not seems to be associated with sorrow or pain or anguish of some sort. The psalmist says, "Weeping may tarry for the night, but joy comes with the morning" (Ps 30:5). And the writer to the Hebrews says that Jesus endured the cross and despised the shame because of the joy set before him. (Heb 12:2). Another illustration is given of a mother suffering pain to produce her newborn child, and the ensuing joy. Jesus is well aware that life has its sorrows. Often for the believer there would be persecution, and always there would be the pressure to conform. He anticipated division and misunderstanding. But for the believer there is the joy — that constant source of encouragement and assurance of what lies ahead. What does cause joy?

In Luke 10 Jesus sends out the twelve, two by two, on a tour of preaching and healing. They must have been diffident about going, and somewhat afraid (Lk 10:17–19). When they return to report to Jesus all that has happened, they can scarcely contain themselves. They are filled with joy. "Even the demons are subject to us in your name" (Lk 10:17). But Jesus recognizes the danger of pride and the lust for power, and warns them not to rejoice in this. "Rejoice," he says, "that your names are written in heaven." To rejoice in commanding the demons may end in bringing glory to myself. Real joy comes in a growing relationship between me and my God (Lk 10:21–22). To be enlisted into the family of God by faith in Christ is the source of joy.

So it is that joy is not dependent upon circumstances. St Paul could say (2 Cor 6:9–10) that he was unknown and yet known by all; he was dead and yet very much alive; he was punished and not killed; he was sorrowful and yet always rejoicing; he was poor and yet making many rich; he had nothing and yet possessed all things.

Behind us and around us and out ahead of us is God's will and purpose. To be part of that will and purpose will change our lives. And it will bring joy. There may be pain and sorrow and loss and disappointment. But these will not disturb the joy. No person or circumstance can take this from us. In Acts 16:23–25 we read of the terrible situation in which Paul and Silas find themselves. Beaten and ill-treated and unjustly dealt with, they are able at midnight in prison to pray and sing hymns of praise to God. This is an expression of pure joy.

For reflection

The secular mind says, "Thank God it's Friday." The person in Christ says, "This is the day that the Lord hath made. We will rejoice and be glad in it." What is your experience of this?

31 Friday

John 16:25–28

Two people can go together to hear Bach's Passion according to St Matthew. They are about the same age; they are both intelligent; they have some interests in common. But one finds the singing of the passion completely beyond him. He is restless and bored throughout the performance. The other person is transported into another world. He is absorbed with the music and the way in which the great story is presented. The difference between the two people is that one is tuned to the message of the word and music. The other is not. For one it is full of meaning. For the other it is unintelligible.

Right at the edge of our sight and understanding are things to be seen and heard and experienced. These are deep things which Jesus is explaining to those who love him. They have just begun to realize and dimly understand some of these truths. Generally to the secular mind they are unintelligible. Jesus speaks of

— the reality of prayer
— the dynamic of faith
— the practical possibility of peace of mind.

So much of this life militates against our growing in this direction. There is the tug of this world; there are the sensual pleasures, the lure of success, all that the world admires and considers so desirable. And all the time Jesus points us to something better, something infinitely more worthwhile. He points to an area beyond sight and sound communicated by the Spirit of God and putting us in touch with abundant living. In this passage Jesus refers to the reality of prayer (16:24).

Jesus is talking to Jews. They are men who have been praying one way or another all their lives. Like us and our prayer book they had their psalms and their liturgy. But Jesus opens up for them and for us a new dimension of prayer. As we hear him speak, we catch the sense of being at the edge of great possibilities. Here is given a new way of approaching the Father. Now it is to be done through a personal relationship with the Son by the power of the Holy Spirit. It is a new era in the experience of prayer. You can stand at the counter in a government office and make a request to see someone through an impersonal bureaucrat. You are not optimistic about your chance. Or, on the other hand, you can claim a close relationship and be ushered immediately into that person's office. Then it is that the possibility of your needs being met become very real and you have a new confidence.

So we pray, making our request with the name of Jesus on our lips. We begin to prove that what he has promised is true. But our desire is to be in his will and no other. Here one finds the reality of prayer.

For reflection

When do you find prayer most real and effective?

32 Saturday

John 16:29–33

Faith can be nebulous and uncertain. You have met people who have faith in tomorrow or faith in human nature. I suppose it is possible to have faith in faith. But faith must have basis in fact. I remember reading a newspaper editorial on Easter Eve which said that Easter affirms our faith in the human spirit. Now all our experience of human spirit does not invite faith. The human spirit is apt to be self-centred and perverse. The human spirit is quite unreliable. Our confidence and faith on Easter Eve lies in the sovereign God who raised Jesus from the dead. The indomitable spirit of humanity will fail us. But the Spirit of God is the place to build trust.

How often I have stood at a hospital bed and discussed with the patient the hope for a quick recovery! And how often I have heard expressed faith in the doctor, faith in the ability to cope physically, faith in miraculous medication! And how often I have had to remind the patient that our faith must be in Jesus Christ and in his healing purpose for us. So it is that Jesus talks with love and conviction in this passage, about the reality of prayer and about the dynamic of faith. And finally (v 33) he talks about the practical possibility of peace.

We live in a threatening world. We are well informed about the horrors on the other side of the world. Some people refuse to read or watch the news; it is too disturbing. They wish that it would go away, and there is much anxiety. And now we read Jesus' prophecy about tribulation (v 33). We know that this has been true for many believers. They have suffered for the cause of Christ and have had to endure persecution.

But what about us in this land of tolerance and religious freedom? Perhaps a better translation for the Greek word *thlipsis* is the word *pressure*. "In this world you will experience pressure," says Christ. And we know what it means. It means going against the stream, it means a refusal to conform to surrounding lifestyles, it means being like Christ rather than like those we work and live with. Jesus lived in the middle of this kind of world. He knew about the pressures and the anxieties and the menacing things. While he was speaking these very words, he knew that some were plotting his death.

Once again into this nervous, anxious, menacing world of ours — a world in which we must live and work — Jesus says, "Be of good cheer. I am in control. I have overcome." And he gives the assurance of peace to those who trust him. He does not offer freedom from pressure but peace in the midst of pressure. It is with this assurance that we can greet each new day.

For reflection

What are the possibilities of interpreting these promises as an escape from the responsibilities of life in Christ? How do we deal with this?

33 Sunday (Lent 5)

John 17:1–5

Now we begin what is generally known as the high priestly prayer. Here Jesus consecrates himself to the great task of redemption which lies immediately ahead of him. There are three sections to the prayer:

(vv 1–5) Jesus prays for himself,
(vv 6–19) Jesus prays for his disciples,
(vv 20–26) Jesus prays for the church.

You learn a lot about people when you hear them pray. Here we are given the privilege of hearing Christ at prayer. Here in this prayer we see into the very mind of Christ. Here the secrets of his heart are unlocked.

He begins by the simple word *Father*. How naturally he turns to God. He is quite at home with God. He moves into his presence with confidence and trust. We see this when a child breaks into his father's presence to make a request or tell him some good news, or to express some sorrow. The child never questions that he will be accepted or loved and listened to. So it is with Christ.

You will find two petitions here. You do not find Christ begging that the course of events might be changed and that he might be spared the cross. He announces that the hour has come. Numerous times before, Jesus had said that his hour had not come. Now it is here. The whole purpose for his coming is at hand. His teaching, his life, his healing, his dealing with people is all prelude to what is about to happen. It is his death, and he prays first that the glory of God may glorify the Son. This was discussed in John 12:28. The glory of God is the character of God. Now Jesus prays that the character may be seen in him at the cross. Here will be the focal point of the revelation of God as seen in Christ. What a request! That through the agony and horror and cruelty and thirst and loneliness he might reflect the goodness and the love of God.

The second request is that it might result in eternal life for all who turn to him. What is eternal life? It is not ours by natural birth. It is not discovered by any searching of ours. It does not become ours by great moral or spiritual effort. It is a gift of God. It is to know God and Jesus Christ, the one sent by God (v 3). How do we know God whom we cannot see? Jesus has declared him and has made it possible for us to know him.

Consider again those two requests. First, the love of God would be seen through the cross. Consider how that prayer was so wonderfully answered.

> See, from his head, his hands, his feet,
> Sorrow and love flow mingled down;
> Did e'er such love and sorrow meet,
> Or thorns compose so rich a crown?

Isaac Watts

Consider the second request — that the cross might result in eternal life for all who turn to him. How has this request been fulfilled? Countless thousands can bear witness to the result of that prayer.

For reflection

What response has my heart made to God's love in Christ?

34 Monday

John 17:6–10

Jesus now begins to pray for his disciples. And as he prays we begin to see the divine plan unfold. It is important for us to know what God has in mind for his world. Here is no *deus ex machina* which dominated theological thinking in the eighteenth century. There is no room here for thinking of God who has wound up the universe to run by itself and who has detached himself from it. Here is a God who visits the earth and makes known the plan.

The plan is that God might make himself known to men and women. Here is the atonement process through which Jesus draws men and women to God. Here and through the passion and death on the cross we see what God is doing. He is in Christ reconciling the world unto himself. God shows himself in Christ. Christ now would show himself in the life of the believer (v 10). All I have is yours, and all you have is mine; and my glory is shown in them.

That is still God's plan. He declares himself in Christ. We see this revelation through his word. We respond by belief and obedience. And God uses us to continue to demonstrate the revelation of himself. Everything else must work to this end. Sacrament and liturgy and church building and structure are ways and means of God introducing people to Christ and revealing the transformed Christ-like life to the world. This is the plan, and Jesus prays that it may indeed happen.

A missionary was sent into the interior of a remote country to a tribe who had never been reached before. He arrived and through an interpreter began describing Jesus, his love, his compassion, his sacrifice. "O, but we have met him" they exclaimed. "Three years ago he was here living with us. He got sick and died and we buried him. But he was exactly like this Jesus you describe." They had met God's revelation of himself in the life of someone who believed Christ and obeyed him and was changed into his image. Here is God's solution to a world longing for love and caring and compassion. It lies with the church and its members who, because they love Christ and trust Christ, find themselves with the marvellous responsibility of presenting him to others.

The story is told of Jesus after the Ascension returning to his heavenly home. He was met by the archangel Michael who inquired about the plan for the church. Jesus told him of the twelve he had selected and whose hearts he had captured and whom he had commissioned to carry on as believing and obedient followers. It now depended upon them. "And if they fail. . .?" asked Michael. "I have no other plan," said Christ.

For reflection

If God's plan is to communicate himself and his love to the world, how do you see yourself as part of that plan?

35   Tuesday
John 17:11–19

There are three petitions in this passage as Jesus prays for his disciples and ultimately for his whole church. They are petitions that we should pray regularly for our church. They are essential prayers if the church is to be the church.

1   The first petition occurs here and recurs later in the passage. It is that the believers may be one (vv 11, 21). He even suggests that the unity in the church resembles the unity between the Son and the Father. Harmony of will and purpose is implied here. A loving relationship is also understood. And the sorry fact is that the church has been known more for its disunity than its unity. The body of believers has been torn apart and has shown anything but the love and the unity for which Christ prays.

The fact that the prayer for unity in the church comes first would indicate the paramount importance of church members being drawn together in trust and gratefulness and loving support. It is an essential hallmark of Christ's church.

2   The second petition concerns the relationship of the believer to the world he lives in (vv 11–16). It is a world that is not reconciled to God. It is hostile to the gospel of Jesus Christ. It is a world that has lost its way. It is a world that rejects the Christ. And yet it is a world that must be reached and confronted by Christ.

Here was the dilemma that Christ had to face. He could take the path of the ascetic and withdraw from the world. But there would be no reconciliation this way. On the other hand he could identify with the world but lose his unique identity. There would be no reconciliation this way either. So it was that Christ walked the dangerous path of being in the world but not of it. And it led him to the cross.

This too is the dilemma of the believer, to be in the world and not of it. He must be identified with the pain and sorrow and heartache of the world but must separate himself from its sin. A dangerous walk indeed! It too involved misunderstanding and scorn and the cross. So Christ prays that, if the church is to be the church and God is to reveal himself, it must be this way.

How is it to be done? What about our appetites, our cravings, our ambitions? St Paul says that the only way is for us to pull down every proud obstacle that is raised against the knowledge of God and take every thought captive and make it obey Christ (2 Cor 10:5).

3   Then comes the third petition. Christ sees the need for the unity of the whole church. He sees the need also for the believer to be in the world but not of it. And then he sees the stunning result of all this and prays for it, that the church may turn the world upside down. Think of it! The supreme goal is that the world may believe. And in believing we will obey, and in obeying the word we will ourselves be transformed into the image of Christ.

This is Jesus' prayer. Such is the prayer that Christ makes for the twelve and for us.

For reflection

How is it possible to be involved in the world, in its politics, its business, its agony, and yet show the character of Christ?

36 *Wednesday*

John 17:20–26

The final verses of this chapter speak to us with special force because now Jesus is praying for us. He says, "I pray for those who believe in me through their word." Anyone who has accepted Christ with apostolic faith is included in this prayer.

Just recently I met a friend whom I had not seen for a long time but who gladdened my heart with these encouraging words, "I never fail to pray for you each day." This reassuring word indicated to me that my friend was sharing my problems with me and assuming some responsibility for them. We should be eternally grateful for the people in Christ who pray for us faithfully.

Now here is Jesus praying for us and, in so doing, assuming concern and responsibility for us and our problems. We are told in scripture that Jesus always lives to make intercession for us (Heb 7:25). This is a great mystery, but it certainly means that we are a concern to him and he enfolds us in his love. Notice what he prays for us.

1   That we should be close to him. How easy it is for us to keep him at a distance! How easy it is to lose touch because of the importance of other things! And we wander off into a far country. Then, spiritually exhausted and poverty stricken, we head home only to find the Father running to meet us. So we read "Draw near to God and he will draw near to you" (Jas 4:8).

2   The result of coming close to Christ is that we might be drawn close to one another. Consider other people as the spokes of a wheel and Christ as the centre. As we move toward him, we must of necessity move closer to one another. Experience shows that the awareness of the presence of Christ

draws us closer to others. As the twelve disciples are drawn to Jesus, they find that with all their barriers and differences Matthew the tax gatherer can embrace Simon the Zealot. This is Christ's prayer: that we love one another and care for one another, differences and all.

3   And then Christ prays for us, that his glory may be seen and reflected. We talked about the glory of God as reflected in Christ in an earlier chapter. We read that the glory of God was revealed in Christ. And we concluded that the glory of God is in his character, his love, his beauty; all this was seen fully in Christ. And now Christ prays that it may be seen in us so that the world may see the glory of God and be won to him.

This prayer is born of a breath-taking vision. Christ in us, we close to him, we close to each other, the world seeing the result. This is Christ's prayer for us. May our prayer this day be

Let the beauty of Jesus be seen in me,
All its wondrous compassion and purity.
O, thou Spirit divine, all my nature refine
Till the beauty of Jesus be seen in me.

Helen Lemmel

For reflection

Can you think of someone today whom your life can touch with healing and love?

37 Thursday

John 18:1–11

The meditative passages of John 13–17 are concluded, and as we enter chapter 18, the pace quickens and the most critical moment in history approaches. Here we are seeing the nature of God and what he is really like on one hand, and the nature of humanity left to its own devices on the other. Here we see in increasing intensity the marvellous love and patience of God. He is prepared to go to any lengths to bring us to himself and to overcome the separation between God and human kind. Here also we see humanity, proud and self-reliant, independent of God and defying him. Judas now attracts our attention. The gospel of John leaves many gaps. You have to read the other gospels to learn that the betrayal was done with a kiss, that the sum of money that changed hands was about twenty-five dollars, that Judas came to a tragic end.

What sort of a man was Judas? Our Lord saw great promise in him and selected him to be one of the twelve. Judas was captured by Christ and was prepared to leave all and follow him. Although John suggests that he pilfered from the common purse, the fact was that when Jesus said, "One of you shall betray me," no one thought of Judas. He must have won their trust, and even to the end our Lord must have hoped it would all turn out differently. Such patience! Such love!

Perhaps we should reflect for a moment on God's high hopes for us. Our beginning was at the font where we were claimed for Jesus Christ and declared a child of God, a member of Christ, and an inheritor of the kingdom. All through the years there was Christian upbringing and the church with its word and sacrament. Are there signs of betrayal? Is it possible that we could put our wishes before his? Or would we trade a close relationship with Christ for some trifling bauble? God knows that it happens every day. Any one of the twelve was capable of betrayal, and they knew it as they asked, "Lord, is it I?"

Sometime during those three precious years with Christ, Judas began to lose touch and his own will became more important than Christ's. There would have been no betrayal had his relationship with the Lord been right. Is there a possibility that I should betray my Lord? Yes, indeed. The seeds of betrayal live with the self-will. But if the self is surrendered to Christ each day and the cross taken up, there will be no betrayal.

Finally, we should remember that Judas's greatest folly lay in taking his own life rather than seeking forgiveness.

There's a wideness in God's mercy
Like the wideness of the sea;
There's a kindness in his justice
Which is more than liberty.
There is no place where earth's sorrows
Are more felt than up in heaven;
There is no place where earth's failings
Have such kindly judgment given.

F.W. Faber

For reflection

Can you picture a different end for Judas, one where he seeks out Jesus and asks for forgiveness? Can you see it happening?

38 Friday

John 18:12–18

Judas and his tragedy yesterday; Simon Peter and his today, as we follow him into the courtyard. Is this John the writer who consistently calls himself that other disciple and never mentions himself by name? He has some entree into the court and introduces the impetuous Simon who has probably coaxed him (v 15). You would have thought that the words of warning coming from our Lord (13:38) would be still ringing in Simon's ears. Had Simon remembered them, he would not have been so eager.

But he is taken by surprise. A servant girl recognizes his accent. One of the soldiers in the guard is related to Malchus, whose ear Simon cut off in the scuffle in the garden. Who would ever have thought of it! But Simon is caught on his blind side, and almost before he knows it he is in trouble. It is so strange that Simon can muster enough courage to attack the guard with a sword, but when he is challenged by the servant girl he has no courage at all. It is a vivid picture of a man or a woman attempting to do what is right in his own strength. This is the same man who thought it was a good idea to jump into the deep water to go to Christ and found himself sinking. This is the same man who acknowledged Jesus as the Christ but refused to have any part in the cross. He would detach himself and make decisions on his own. At this stage of his pilgrimage he is quite unreliable, and the Lord turned and looked at Peter, and Peter went out and wept bitterly (Lk 22:61–62).

Presently the Holy Spirit will come upon the church, and we need never be detached from the Lord again. We need no longer be "on our own" crusading for irresponsible causes and then acting as if we never knew Christ. For the power of the

Holy Spirit can bind us in union with the Lord and with one another. It is the Holy Spirit that strengthens the heart and deepens the love so that we need not be thrown into disarray by some challenge.

Let us begin each day open to the Spirit of God, and then let us face the issues of the day. You will not be challenged by some maid in some court yard. But you may suddenly have to make a decision which will make clear whether you are one of Christ's or whether you are on your own. It may be a moral decision. It may affect your relationship with those you love. It may involve considerable sacrifice on your part as you declare yourself to be "one of his." And you will know very quickly whether there has been betrayal or denial. You may even sense that Christ is looking at you with love and concern.

But it is the Holy Spirit that assures our closeness to Christ. May we be faithful to him and may the people who challenge us never be in any doubt that we are one of his.

For reflection

From what area do you see your loyalty to Christ challenged?

39 Saturday

John 18:19–27

What was your reaction to the reading of verse 22? Did your blood boil as the picture was given of the officer striking the helpless prisoner with his hand? Did you have an involuntary desire to punish this officer for his outrageous act? Your response is quite natural. If we read Acts 23:2–4 we find how Paul reacted to this kind of treatment. And all our sympathies are with Paul. He had every right to lash out as he did.

But Jesus, under the most provocative conditions, refuses to over-react. He is under control and shows forgiveness at the most unlikely situations. The same sort of response will presently be demonstrated on the cross when Jesus says to those who mocked him and tortured him, "Father, forgive them for they know not what they do." We are apt to dismiss this marvellous self-control and willingness to forgive. We say that, of course, Jesus would do this because of who he is. We forget that he felt the outrage and the pain just as sharply as we do. An act of injustice did not touch him with any less pain than it does us. To believe other than this would be to deny his humanity.

How we need the mind of Christ! Because of selfish interests we over-react. We are sensitive about what is said about us, and we "blow up" when we encounter injustice. The mind of Christ overcomes the threat and the twisting of the truth and the "put-down," and simply forgives. If to love is to know, then our Lord knows what is in the minds of these people — the cross currents, the sense of failure, the arrogance that hides inner collapse. And through this whole outrage he sees their need. And he loves them and reaches out to them.

Nothing less is expected of those who are Christ's and who have the Spirit of Christ. "Let this mind be in you which was in Christ Jesus." And so we pray for each encounter this day, "Lord, keep me from over-reacting." "Lord, help me to understand why he is doing what he is doing." "Lord, teach me to love even where there is no love in return."

Such love will help us to understand. And such understanding will produce forgiveness. And all of it is the work of the Holy Spirit which filled the life of Jesus.

For reflection

What are we to say about those natural reactions of ours in the home and in the work place? After all, are they not simply human reactions?

40 Sunday Of The Palm

John 18:28–32

Were it not such a tragic moment in this passage the inconsistency of the leaders of religion would be laughable. Imagine their keeping impeccably the religious law, lest they be defiled and disqualified from eating the Passover, and at the same time venting their anger upon the one who would be our Passover, sacrificed for us.

I suspect that there is the same kind of inconsistency in our own lives. We make sure we are in time for the communion service and then abstain because the celebrant is black or a woman. Such contradictions plague our lives, and we may well be unaware of them. If the mind is closed and the eye of the soul blinded, there will be inconsistencies. Our Lord speaks of this with great force in Matthew 23.

This kind of inconsistency, which we have named Pharisaism, is the disease of the devoted. It belongs to people who started with a worthy goal. But in pursuing this goal they have become preoccupied with the means and have lost sight of the original end. To glorify God and to enjoy him forever is a worthy goal and has been accepted by the church as the chief end of humanity. One of the ways of glorifying God is to remember the Sabbath day to keep it holy. But when the keeping of the Sabbath day becomes an end in itself, then the glorifying of God may become secondary and even forgotten.

What is the most important goal in life for you? It may be quite selfish. It may be to climb to the top of the business ladder or the social ladder. It may be to win academic excellence or to see it happen in your children. But if we were created by God and for God, we may view life in terms of our relationship with Jesus Christ. This relationship must be nurtured and guarded.

It is possible that, in doing things designed to strengthen the relationship, we may fall into the trap of the Pharisees and lose sight of the goal altogether. We may become so concerned with the shape and practice of the liturgy that we forget what it means to feed on Christ by faith with thanksgiving. It is quite possible for us in our concern about form to forget the substance.

So it is that the Saviour speaks to us, the devoted. He recognizes where our concern lies. He sees us absorbed with prayer book revision, liturgical reform, peace marches, liberation of oppressed peoples. He recognizes the soundness of the cause. But he longs for a deepening personal relationship with the believer. His deepest wish is to make us like himself. This we must face first in our priorities for today.

Let this be our prayer: "Lord, what do you want me to do?" But be careful in asking it. You will find yourself on the road to the cross, the place of self-sacrifice.

For reflection

Have you a particular cause or interest which might inhibit your relationship to Christ?

41 Monday

John 18:33–40

We sense in reading this story that Pilate would have given much to escape having to make a decision about Jesus. The historians tell us that he is already in trouble with the authorities in Rome because of political unrest in Jerusalem. He must avoid a disturbance. And yet that is what lies ahead if he does not listen to the religious rulers. On the other hand he sees the personal enmity of the same leaders against the prisoner Jesus and their unjust case against him. He is caught in a forked stick and cannot really move one way or another.

The fact is that Pilate is very confused at this moment. There are many questions for which he would like to know the answers. Is there a God? Is there absolute truth and, if so, how does one find it and know it? And then, these religious people who claim to be in touch with God, why do they display such hatred for one of their own kinfolk? Life is puzzling, and there are many unanswerables. How many countless people would like to know the answer to the question, Who am I? or to the question, How do I know who is right?

Do you suppose that Pilate, caught in his own uncertainties, sensed a new and fresh certainty in Jesus? When Jesus said, "I am the way, the truth, and the life," he introduced a whole new level of certainty and conviction. You can sense this as you read Paul's letter to the Romans. Paul must have shared Pilate's uncertainties at one time. But new life in Christ gave him absolute certainty about who he was and where he was going. In his academic world of conjecture and guess work, it is only the person in Christ who can say, "We know that in everything God works for good with those who love him" (Rom 8:28).

It would seem that, like Pontius Pilate, people today are paralyzed by fear and uncertainty. If you don't know who you are, you may well be at a loss when it comes to moral decisions or certain direction.

But, if you are a child of God by faith in Christ Jesus, some things will become certainties in your life, as we read in 1 John.

1 we know that we have eternal life (1 Jn 5:13);
2 we know that God hears and responds to our prayer (1 Jn 5:15);
3 we know that the believer in Christ is emancipated from the power of sin (1 Jn 5:18);
4 we know that the believer in Christ is aligned with God's purpose for the world (1 Jn 5:19);
5 we know and see what the unbelieving world cannot know or see (1 Jn 5:20).

It was at the close of a parish mission, which I was asked to conduct, that a man waited at the door to speak to me. His question to me was this: "How can you be so sure?" no doubt referring to a sermon just given with some conviction. My response to him was that, when a person places trust in Christ, and builds up some knowledge of the scriptures, and is open to the work of the Holy Spirit, then that person possesses unshakable certainties that give strength and confidence to face the issues of life.

For reflection

Read 2 Timothy 1:12. Where does St Paul's confidence come from? Have we a right to the same confidence?

42 *Tuesday*

John 19:1–11

Now it is that we see the whole world on trial. To be sure it is Jesus who is interrogated and mocked and flogged and finally crucified. But it is really Pilate and the whole world whom he represents who are on the prisoner's stand.

When Martin Luther faced the Diet of Worms and declared, "Here I stand, I can do no other," it was clearly obvious that the court rather than the prisoner was on trial. In the case of each trial of this sort you find people detaching themselves from the heavy responsibility. Pilate's wife sends a message to her husband bidding him to have nothing to do with this just man (Mt 27:19). Pilate washes his hands in full view of the people. No one wants to be involved.

But in this passage everyone is inescapably involved. At the time they made every effort to detach themselves. Pilate would declare to those about him that he had no choice. The soldiers would say that they were doing only their duty. The disciples who forsook him and fled would say that there was no sense staying around. But twenty centuries later we are singing:

> I see the crowds in Pilate's hall,
> Their furious cries I hear;
> Their shouts of 'Crucify' appal,
> Their curses fill my ear.
> And of that shouting multitude
> I feel that I am one,
> And in that din of voices rude
> I recognize my own.

Horatius Bonar

The trial continues. Men and women are still asking who Jesus is. Mocking and scourging are carried on daily as Jesus is crucified afresh. And for the most part people avoid responsibility. If Jesus is there, they don't want to be there; for to be where he is is to be strangely drawn in and involved.

But worldly minded people avoid this. They live in a private condominium and do not even want to know the names of the people in their building. They vaguely suspect that someone at work is having troubles, but they avoid asking any questions lest they be involved. The sick and the infirm, the prisoner and the beggar remind them of problems that are not theirs. And in their non-involvement they are joining in the flogging and the mockery just as surely as Pilate.

So it is that there are no bystanders or onlookers in our passage. And the question confronts us all, "What then will you do with Jesus who is called the Christ?"

For reflection

Read St Matthew 25:40–45. What is the conviction between this passage and the question, "What will you do with Jesus?"

43   Wednesday

John 19:12–16

We watch with awe and amazement as we see Pilate losing control of the whole process of justice. The time when he could step in and stop this nonsense has passed, and there is a kind of inevitability about the proceedings. The storm cloud that appeared in chapter 12 is now black and threatening. Nothing will save Jesus from the cross.

I was conducting a conference of Christian students at which two non-believers were present. I wanted to draw them into the discussion, and I asked them what would happen were Jesus to appear in the city proclaiming the kingdom and healing and demonstrating what we see in the gospels. The two students were silent for a moment, and then one of them said, "We would kill him, of course."

Is it possible? Surely not! But holy scripture says, "A person becomes an enemy of God when he is controlled by human nature (Rom 8:7). What is happening here is the universal human drama. When a worldly person is confronted by God, there is enmity between the two. It is all anticipated in the early records where man and woman are seen hiding from God, where they are seen working out a lifestyle separated from God. At the very beginning of history they say, "Let us make a tower with its top in the heavens, and let us make a name for ourselves" (Gen 11:4).

Nothing makes any sense of the crucifixion of Jesus until we remember that there is alienation between humanity and God. And when we hear the shouts of "crucify him" and the mocking and the flogging, we see the culmination of this hatred. Surely the Lord has laid on him the iniquity of us all. (Is 53:6).

It is the lowest moment in the experience of all humanity, and as we stand dumbfounded and helpless, we know that only God could produce blessing unlimited out of this black scene. For as our Christ takes upon himself our alienation and our rejection and our sin, he invites us to meet him at the cross for forgiveness and healing and new life. The blackest moment of history is to become the brightest moment. He became sin for us that we might be set free. Praise God! He is faithful and just to forgive us our sin and to cleanse us from all iniquity.

Pilate loses control but God takes control. The irresponsibility of man becomes the responsibility of God so that two thousand years after that black day we are still singing

> In the Cross of Christ I glory,
> Towering o'er the wrecks of time;
> All the light of sacred story
> Gather round its head sublime.
>
> *Sir John Bowring*

For reflection

If the way of the cross represents suffering and surrender and sacrifice and dying, how is it possible to glory in it?

44 Thursday

John 19:17–24

How carefully this story is told but with an economy of words. We see in this passage Jesus carrying his own cross. Many artists have tried to depict his resolve, his suffering, his compassion. It is the absolute watershed of history. For this very moment was he born, and everything he did and said finds its meaning right here. Atonement is his purpose, cost what it may. His passion is to see atonement coming from the cross. With one hand he will reach out from that cross and take the hand of God, and with the other he will reach down and take my hand and yours and anyone who looks to him in faith; and through his death he will bring God and man together. He is the at *One*-ment. "God was in Christ reconciling the world unto himself" (2 Cor 5:19).

It was more than a heroic death. It was more than a loving sacrifice. It was God's way of dealing with sin, with pride, with self, with the separating thing. St Paul comes close to the mystery when he says, "For our sake God made him to be sin who knew no sin, so that in him we might become the righteousness of God (2 Cor 5:21). Here are the benefits of his passion. It is a brand new beginning. All the cries of despair and doubt and disappointment which are heard in the story of the Old Testament and in the experience of human kind find some answer at the cross.

I was peering through the nursery window at a beautiful newborn baby when a rough, earthy, unsentimental man stood beside me sharing the same view. "Lucky kid," he said to me. "Wouldn't you just love to be able to start over with everything all fresh and new?" And I realized that I was hearing the cry of his heart and the universal cry of humanity. Here is the longing of the heart, the really deep need — not to win the lottery, not to be a success in business, not to have the office on the corner with wall to wall carpet and the key to the private washroom, not even to see your children a success. The real longing is to be able to start again. The deep need is to be forgiven and to know that things are right with God.

All this and much more must have been in Jesus' mind as he carried his cross. For him the greatest joy was to see alienated humanity reconciled to his God. It was the joy of seeing a person in Christ becoming brand new. And because of that joy he endured the cross and despised the shame.

As we view these events, we are witness to the greatest tragedy of history. And yet it is not that, for God made of it blessed redemption. No, the greatest tragedy of history is that it all may have happened in vain. St Paul in 1 Corinthians 6:1 suggests such a possibility, and reminds us as we view the passion, of the need to respond with open and grateful heart.

For reflection

In what ways might the grace of God be received in vain (2 Cor 6:1)?

45 Friday

John 19:25–37

Seven statements are recorded for us from the cross, and St John gives us three of them. The final one, "It is finished," would leave no question mark in the minds of the faithful. They had hoped for something else, for some divine intervention, for those twelve legions of angels to come and deliver him. It had all been so promising, so faithful to Old Testament prophecy, and so convincing. What could they say about the people healed of their diseases and the lives blessed? Life would never be the same again for them. And now it is finished. The dream is over.

But it is Jesus himself who says "It is finished." He had spoken of rising from the dead. He had spoken clearly that the disciples would do greater works than he. He talked of the tremendous events yet to be experienced. What, then, does he mean by "It is finished"?

We sense relief in that cry, the racking pain of the cross, the trials and disappointments of life, the separation from the Father. They are finished and it is a cry of relief.

This must also be a cry of victory. We know that he was beset by the evil one. Time and time again he was tempted and tried. Some of the struggle is seen in the wilderness, some in the garden as he shrank from the ordeal of pain and separation ahead. We can only dimly guess the struggle as the crowd pressed in on him to make him king. Those were no easy struggles as he stood with his back to the wall. So much depended upon his overcoming the tempter if he were to be the Lamb of God that takes away the sin of the world. But now it is finished, and he has gained the victory.

This cry was also a message to the Father. I have finished the work which you gave me to do. What was that work? It was to reveal the Father and his purpose of grace. It was to manifest God's holiness and love. It was to bear in his own body the penalty for sin. It was to make atonement and to link humanity with God in a new relationship. This is the finished work which never needs to be repeated. We find our lives finishing with so little done and so much still to do. Only Christ knew the exultation of having finished his own work.

Finally, his cry of "It is finished" is a proclamation to men and women. It says that the final revelation of God to humanity has been given. It says that the alienation between God and humanity has been healed. And it says that now the kingdom of heaven is open to all believers.

So we stand in wonder and praise. We are amazed that Pilate lost control. Everything that happens seems to be in the plan of God. The seamless garment is not torn. Not a bone of his body is broken. In the midst of injustice run riot there is a kind of order about it all. And a new creation is born in Christ. Thanks be to God.

For reflection

How happy to be able to say, "It is finished," at the end of a life. There is a clue to this sense of fulfilment in St Matthew 25:19-21. What is it?

46 Saturday
John 19:38–42

What was happening while Jesus lay in the tomb? In 1 Peter 3:19 there is a vague reference to Christ's preaching to the spirits in prison. It has been suggested that Jesus presented the good news of reconciling grace to the faithful who lived and died before the cross. What a dramatic picture that conjures up before us!

But there is another dramatic picture given us here of the secret negotiations between Joseph of Arimathea and Pilate, that Jesus might be given a burial with love and dignity. And then, almost by chance, we run across Nicodemus again. You will remember our first encounter with him when he comes to Jesus by night to discuss spiritual matters. It is at that time (3:1) that Jesus opens up to Nicodemus the possibility of being born of the Spirit and becoming a new creation in Christ. You may have wondered what happened to Nicodemus. Was he genuinely seeking that quality of life that he saw in Jesus? And did he leave the interview a believer?

He turns up again in John 7:50 where he is challenged to break out of his secret inquiry and show open sympathy for Jesus and his cause. And now we see him once again in this passage for today. Everyone has forsaken Christ and is in hiding. It is dangerous for anyone associated with the Lord to be seen in public. And at that most dangerous moment Nicodemus comes out into the public and identifies himself as one who belongs to Jesus Christ, no matter what the cost may be. What a lovely story — to see him change from secret inquirer to public sympathizer to someone who wants nothing else than to be identified with Christ and to belong to him.

The story of Nicodemus challenges us at our point of faithfulness to the Lord Christ. Where are we when the unbelieving world mocks and scorns and treats our Lord with cool contempt? Where are we when the hungry one and the naked, the homeless and the prisoner appear before us and are shown dear to the heart of Christ? Are we there identifying with the death of Christ, ourselves nailed to the cross, our reputation at stake, our wealth and time and energy ready to be offered? Are we really ready to sing

Love so amazing, so divine
Demands my soul, my life, my all.

For reflection

Can you, like Nicodemus, recall definite stages of growth in your relationship to Christ? Where are you now?

47 Easter Day

John 20:1–9

It was originally intended that these studies and reflections conclude at the end of John 19. The hope was that, if it were a Lenten series, all who read might proceed to the eucharist on Easter Day and greet the risen Lord. However, if these studies are used in other ways, they might appear incomplete without a reflection upon the great news of the risen Christ.

We find ourselves at the scene, so vividly is it told. Mary Magdalene and then Peter and John make the second great discovery of their lives. The first is that God is in Christ, living our life, feeling our infirmities, sharing our sorrows, and identifying with us in every way. And now the second discovery that this Jesus, born of God, suffered, died, and has been raised from the dead. Death could not hold him. He is alive for ever more. Here is the keystone of our faith. We rejoice in his life, his teaching, his miracles, his compassion, his sacrifice. But our faith is in a risen Christ, and it is him we celebrate each Lord's Day as we break bread in eucharist.

Some people deny the Resurrection as an historic fact. St Paul says that their faith is empty and they have no good news. They talk about the example of Christ as eternal, or the memory of Christ or the spirit of Christ living on in human hearts. But nothing has been done for them about death.

I thank God that we have placed centrally in our service of Eucharist that great affirmation

Christ has died.
Christ is risen.
Christ will come again.

It is absolutely basic to our faith for today and our hope for tomorrow that we know that Jesus who died is alive for everyone. More than that, he makes it possible for those who share his life to be alive for ever more. And the message of this Easter Day is that not only is Christ risen but that we can be risen with him. There is no one else in the world saying this except the person in Christ.

Watch carefully the scenes recorded for us following the raising of Jesus from the dead; Mary in the garden, the two on the road to Emmaus, the ten in the upper room, Thomas, Simon Peter, the scene by the sea of Galilee. Always there is amazement and joy as they eventually recognize the risen Lord. He is alive.

It was the Holy Spirit that brought Christ from the grave. It is that same Spirit that will open our eyes to see and acknowledge that Christ is alive and at work in our midst today.

For reflection

What evidence have you for saying that Jesus is alive?